THE HOUSE STANDS FIRM

The House Stands Firm

FAMILY LIFE IN WEST AFRICA

SISTER MARIE-ANDRÉ DU SACRÉ-COEUR, W.S.

TRANSLATED FROM THE FRENCH BY ALBA I. ZIZZAMIA

THE BRUCE PUBLISHING COMPANY
MILWAUKEE

Library of Congress Catalog Card Number: 62–16836

© 1962 THE BRUCE PUBLISHING COMPANY
MADE IN THE UNITED STATES OF AMERICA

Foreword

This is the first time that a book by Soeur Marie-André du Sacré-Coeur is being presented to the American public. The earlier writings of this author have not been translated into English, but they have had a wide distribution among the French-speaking peoples and have had a great influence on European thinking concerning Africa.

The author is indeed one of the few real experts on the life of the Africans, the social structure of their societies and their family relationships as formed under the influence of customs and traditions. During the many years Soeur Marie-André spent in Africa as a White Sister missionary, working particularly with African women, she has come to know and to love this continent and its people. This knowledge and this love are reflected on every page of the present book. The histories of the various families related here are known to the author because she was accepted in these families as one of them, and because her deep understanding of their problems allowed them to confide in her and to seek her guidance and assistance.

The reader of this book will, I think, feel — as I do — that this is not a book written by a European about people in other parts of the world, but the story of the lives of the author's African friends, whether they be Christians, Moslems, or pagans. Soeur Marie-André went to them and lived with them because she wanted to help them and to learn from them. She tells us of the evolution which is taking place at present and of the effects of this evolution on the everyday life of the Africans. The reader will be, with her, a guest at weddings, at funerals, at various celebrations, some of them religious, other tribal. He will learn to understand why the African woman, perhaps more than women of other regions, needs the help of people like Soeur Marie-André in order to achieve recognition of her dignity as a human being and acknowledgment of her status as a citizen of her country and of the world.

I am deeply convinced that this book, which does not state or defend any specific thesis or point of view but which presents to the reader, with disarming simplicity and singular clarity, the complex problems existing in African society today, will be an important instrument for the achievement by all African women of the place which they deserve in that society.

SOPHIE GRINBERG-VINAVER
Chief — Status of Women Section
United Nations

New York
January, 1962

About the Author

Many distinctions have come to Sister Marie-André du Sacré-Coeur in the long years of her life, but perhaps none have meant more to her than her achievements on behalf of African women, most of which are known only to herself and the many who have confided their troubles to her purposeful assistance.

Lawyer, author, and missionary nurse, she was born Jeanne Dorge and grew up in northern France in what she describes simply as a happy Christian family, who encouraged her fondness for study through the stresses and strains imposed by World War I. Her first love was medicine, but when her mother objected to her pursuing it as a profession, she enrolled as a law student at the Institut Catholique in Paris and later went on for her doctorate at the Catholic University in Lille. Her thesis dealt with the problems of abandoned families, a kind of omen for her future activity and later, since it had brought her to the attention of prominent experts on family welfare, it was to become an open sesame to those who could be of most help in her efforts on behalf of African women.

But first Jeanne Dorge put her doctorate behind her, went to Algiers to enter the Missionary Sisters of Our Lady of

Africa — the White Sisters — and in 1927 was professed as Soeur Marie-André du Sacré-Coeur. She studied nursing and from then on, with the inscrutable logic of Providence, medicine and law were interwoven through her next seventeen years as missionary nurse and teacher to make her an acknowledged expert on West African family life and a pioneer in promoting the status of African women.

After a first tour of duty in mission dispensaries in North Africa, she served in various mission clinics throughout the West African countries then under French control. In bush village, market town, and booming port city, through home visits for follow-up treatment, conversations and surveys conducted with affectionate tact, she came to know, respect, and love the women of Africa, "who do so much with so little." Their status of inferiority in customary law aroused the lawyer in her, while the suffering she encountered in the daily round of human problems deeply engaged her compassion.

Her first published work on the subject was *La Femme Noire en Afrique Occidentale* (1939) which created a stir among specialists in African studies. In both Europe and Africa she was the determined advocate of African women, in numerous lectures, articles in a variety of publications, and in presentations before the French Chamber of Deputies, becoming the first woman invited to speak before a committee of that body. Both the *Mandel* (1939) and *Jacquinot* (1951) decrees to which she refers in the present text, incorporated her recommendations. The adoption of both decrees was in fact largely due to the quietly knowledgeable and persistent efforts of Soeur Marie-André and those whose interest her own indomitable concern enlisted in the cause.

In 1949, the Office of Overseas Scientific Research requested Sister Marie-André to do a study of the changes in African family life and the status of women taking place in the postwar years. A sixteen-month study tour in former French West Africa resulted in *La Condition Humaine en Afrique Noire* (1953). Other published works include *Sous le Ciel d'Afrique* (1948) and *Civisation en Marche* (1956). The latter was written after an extensive tour of Uganda, Rwanda, Burundi, and the Congo followed her participation in the first Congress of the Lay Apostolate to be held in Africa (Kisubi, Uganda, 1953).

A particularly interesting feature of Sister Marie-André's first works is the way she has set African customary law within the perspective of our own historical background with an analysis of its similarities to the laws governing the ancient Roman and Teutonic family groups and of traditions and practices similar to those of Western society until the Modern Era.

A frequent participant and speaker at international seminars and conferences, she took part in the *Semaine Internationale d'Etudes* held in Leopoldville in 1955, the *Semaine Internationale Lumen Vitae* at Anvers in August, 1956, and the conference on the African child organized in the Cameroun in January, 1957, by the International Catholic Child Bureau. This last congress she attended as the representative of the World Union of Catholic Women's Organizations, for which she has served as consultant on African matters for several years. She conducted workshops for African women at its Rome congress in 1957, at the UNESCO-sponsored seminar it organized in Lome, Togo, in 1958, and at its international workshop held in Nyasaland in 1961. She also represented the World Union of Catholic

Women's Organizations and St. Joan's Alliance at the 1959 session of the UN Commission on the Status of Women (the first nun to speak before a UN body) and at the UN Seminar on the participation of women in public life, held in December, 1960, in Addis Ababa, Ethiopia.

In addition to her cooperation with women's organizations Sister Marie-André is a member of France's *Academie des Sciences d'Outre-Mer,* and was a member of the *Conseil Superieur des Affaires Sociales d'Outre-Mer* and of the *Conseil Superieur des Recherches Sociologiques d'Outre-Mer* until 1959, when France's overseas territories attained independence.

Her warmhearted kindliness and compassionate interest have won her not only the confidence of the women but also the respect and trust of the men, as her voluminous correspondence with both attests. Her friends are numbered among the new African intellectuals and untutored village girls alike. First claim on her attention is still the hopes, problems, and concerns of women caught between the old and the new in their striving for a fuller life, for numbers of whom she is still confidante, counselor, and moral support.

The title of this book is taken from a Togolese saying, *Apelete,* one word which means "the house stands firm, the wife is within and all is well." In reality it might be applied to all present-day Africa, in whose future the stabilizing influence of women is already playing no small role. It is Sister Marie-André's conviction that their common sense, their loyalty to sound African values and family traditions, and their intelligent appraisal of the new will, despite the upheavals and tensions of transition, ensure that in the new house Africa is now building all will be well.

A. I. Z.

Preface

The true face of Africa is not easy to discover, though not a week goes by but that some sensational news or other is reported in the press, or a panel discussion comes over the radio, or a documentary lights up the television screen. We learn how the Pygmies hunt, we see witch doctors, tribal dances and bright new buildings, or we hear an African delegate addressing the United Nations. But this is not enough to know Africa. . . .

There are excellent books a-plenty, by ethnologists who have lived for long years in a given region and who describe in detail the peoples and their customs, by travelers who know how to observe and to listen, by Africans themselves — poets, novelists, historians — who reveal in clear and concrete fashion the needs, sufferings, and aspirations of their compatriots. Noteworthy among the latter are the poems of Leopold Sedar Senghor — now president of the Republic of Senegal — the books of Camara Laye, Peter Abrahams, and the last novel of Joseph Owono, *Tante Bella,* which describes the unhappy status of Camerounian women.

Yet it seems we still do not know enough about daily life in Africa, about social and family organization, about the work that men do and women do and their reactions to the events that touch all human life — birth, marriage, sickness, death. . . . What are the basic characteristics of their civilization, the religious and moral principles that guide their actions? Have they proverbs that are the distillation of the wisdom of their Ancients? Do they have the disposition to artistic achievement and the refinements of courtesy that are the flowers of a true civilization? And, especially, what is the status of woman among them, her influence in the family, her role with respect to her husband and children? These are important questions, which shape the distinctive features of a people.

There is no general answer to these questions, however, for Africa has far greater diversity than America.

If one were to write about the American family, which would he choose as typical? The farm family of the Middle West, or an average family in Eastern Suburbia? And then whose family would it be — the broker's, the lawyer's, the factory worker's, the white collar worker's . . . ?

Who is the typical American woman — the salesgirl, secretary, school principal, nurse, housewife, socialite, film star, nun? None of them would give us a complete portrait of the American woman. Each would give just one feature.

Just as the various countries of Europe and the Americas share, in broad outline, the same "Western" civilization, the different peoples of Africa have in common a certain basic culture, laws and customs, many elements of which are reminiscent of our Roman or Teutonic ancestors. In our society these ancestral customs have long since been abandoned, owing mainly to the influence of Christianity, which transformed them with the injection of the moral teachings of the Gospels. A similar transformation is taking place in Africa, and it is affecting to see the eagerness with which her young people are reaching out for the change.

There are considerable differences, however, between one African people and another, and even among families within the same region. There are families that might be called "Westernized," but there are also the great majority whose way of life, materially and socially, is still that of their ancestors of the twelfth and thirteenth centuries.

In sub-Saharan Africa, there are no "great fortunes" in the American or European sense. Though the area is economically poor and its resources largely undeveloped, there are families — as everywhere in the world — who are relatively well off and others who are very poor. There are the arrogant and domineering, and the easygoing and compliant. There are those anxious to serve God, respectful of the rights of others; and those less scrupulous who seek only their own advantage or pleasure.

One must also keep in mind differences in historical development and in the geographical conditions which determine to a large extent the daily lives of the various populations. Differences of climate and culture, a rural or an urban background, conversion to Christianity, educational development, the social status of the family, all affect the way of life. The customary way in which most families live in Bamako or Accra is no longer followed in individual families I know in those same towns; and the problem that endangers the future in one region does not exist 500 miles away.

Is it perhaps because of these differences, which make exposition difficult, that questions concerning the daily life of the individual and the family, the evolution of juridical institutions and their influence on social life are little touched upon as a rule? Or is it because one can speak of the customs of a people only with great tact and discretion — and much love?

This book deals particularly with family life. For the face of a people is best reflected in the day-by-day routine that marks their life throughout the year. I have limited myself to the regions of West Africa which I know best, where I lived for many years, caring for the sick at home and at our dispensaries, doing social work among women, studying their customs and the changes slowly taking place in their ways under the influence of Christianity, education, or contact with other cultures.

In my daily rounds I came to know intimately the difficulties they encounter, the unmerited distress which often befalls them and which they wish to spare their children. I was privileged to share their joys and their sufferings, and to understand what made them suffer. We often spoke together of the great problems that are their anxious concern and how best to bring progress to their country. And in heart-to-heart talks, I learned that their personal problems are the same human problems one meets everywhere. The framework is different, shaped by the climate, economic underdevelopment, lack of schooling for the great majority, primitive methods of work, and the distinctive legal and social structures which mark each region.

To set these problems in perspective, it is useful to consider what life has been and is for the people of West Africa, to understand something of the ancient custom that still governs most of them, the changes through which this custom has passed and is still passing, and what the Africans wish to keep of their customary institutions as they adapt them to the modern world.

When we know the Africans better, when we understand their anxieties, their major problems and their daily difficulties, their lawful aspirations and their desire for a standard of living more like our own, our respect and admiration for them increases. With limited resources, amid the unsettling pressures of transition, they are shaping a future of progress in which, while they hopefully select what they think best in non-African civilizations, they intend to remain essentially themselves. But the process means inevitably a rearrangement of their way of life.

This book has no purpose other than to contribute a little to the sympathetic understanding and co-operation which our African brothers and sisters have every right to expect.

Contents

CONTENTS

THE HOUSE STANDS FIRM

1. Daily Life in West Africa

There are in the United States a number of Africans from all over the continent — students, visitors, government sponsored exchangees, diplomats, UN delegates. Until recently most of them have come from the English-speaking countries of East and West Africa. Frequently they have belonged to families of rather high social status, with a standard of living analogous to that of well-to-do or upper middle class America. Most of them are seriously concerned with the progress of their country. As they study, among other things, health services, school systems, economics, administration, social welfare, it is with the intention of returning home to practice — with some adaptation — what they have learned.

What is the West Africa like to which they will return? Geographically it extends over an area of two million square miles, 800,000 of which are above the 17th parallel, or in the Saharan region, inhabited by white races, such as the Maures, Peuhls, Tuaregs. This book, however, deals only with the Negro Africans who live south of that parallel.

Below the Sahara, stretches the savanna, 800,000 square miles of flat expanse, with an occasional mountain or rocky plateau here and there, rising to a height of 1400 to 2000 feet. These plateaux sometimes end abruptly in steep cliffs that overhang the grasslands, or descend gently down a tiered slope to the plain. The savanna is covered with bushes and tall grasses, with a scattering of baobobs, mahogany, shea butter, and silk cotton trees in whose branches nest bright-colored birds of magnificent plumage. South of the savanna, the forest begins, thin at first and then merging into the great equatorial forest teeming with oil palms, kola, banana, and rubber trees, the latter growing as high as 200 feet. The crowding vegetation is so dense that the slender trunks seem to be trying to push through it as high as possible to catch a ray of sunlight. But this forest is gradually disappearing — especially in Dahomey, Ghana, Togo, and Nigeria — as plantations of export crops take over: oil palm, hevea rubber, cocoa, coffee.

The principal West African rivers are the Senegal, the Niger, the Casamance, the Gambia, the Voltas, the Comoe, and the Benue. There are smaller rivers in the forest area, while in the savanna a number of intermittent streams, impassable torrents after a storm, but parched gullies during the dry season — from November to May — during which there isn't a single drop of rain. Only during the rainy season — from May to October — can the peoples of the savanna grow anything, and their main food crop is millet. In the more humid regions below the savanna, maize, rice — where irrigation is possible — cassava, yams, and groundnuts are cultivated.

In the forest region the rains are much more frequent, and here rice and maize together with bananas are the staples in the diet, supplemented with yams and cassava root. Truck gardens are being developed now even in the savanna, wherever it is possible to obtain water.

The Cameroun, east of Nigeria, comprises an area of

2

170,000 square miles. The north is savanna country, with high plateaux, cliffs, volcanic rocks, and the plateau of Adamaoua, which the explorer Barth called one of the most beautiful areas of central Africa. To the west, along the Nigerian border, 13,000-foot Mount Cameroun presides over fertile savanna, and in the south we meet again the great tropical forest. The Camerounian climate and crops are as varied as those in the rest of West Africa. The Cameroun's principal rivers are the Wouri and the Sanaga, which support a large population of hippopotami.

West Africa's rivers are rich in many varieties of fish, a precious source of food for populations in rural areas, who practice little or no husbandry. Scrawny goats and sheep — formerly reserved mostly for sacrifices — and small donkeys are to be found in fair number, but few horses. Chickens and guinea hens have the run of the villages, but their owners do not feed them. They are left to scratch for whatever they can find in the refuse or the bush.

The Peuhls, a shepherd people who live in groupings scattered like islets through the savanna, have herds which are either their personal property or have been entrusted to their care by other tribes, like the Mossi or Bambara. There are, however, other tribes whose members herd their own cattle (i.e., the Gurunsi of Northern Ghana, the Lobi and Dagari of the Upper Volta). But the bulls are not used in farming and the cows are not milked: their milk is left for the young calves. For these tribes, cattle constitute primarily a social asset; they demonstrate the owner's wealth and at times may be offered in sacrifices. But, above all, cattle are a medium of exchange in securing a bride.

The Peuhls do milk their cows, which, nourished by skimpy pasture land, yield only a few pints per day.

3

Most Africans are enthusiastic hunters. Boys get birds with their slings or catch rats, lizards, or snakes, which are broiled and eaten "for meat." Men hunt with bows and arrows, spears, and now with rifles. In the bush, one still comes upon deer, antelopes, monkeys, boars, hares. But it is rare now to meet a lion or panther.

The traditional house is a mud hut, round or rectangular, with a flat clay-covered roof or one of straw thatch. It is always built with great care. Formerly, the only opening was the door, which varied in height from one area to the next, but now many huts also have a window or two. Sometimes there was a small round hole in the roof serving as a chimney.

Every woman has the right to one or two separate rooms for herself and her children (three, in the case of the Gurunsi of Northern Ghana) opening off a small court where she does her cooking and which is circled by a wall two or three feet high. All the houses of the same family are grouped around a large interior court that also encloses conical storage bins. These bins are sometimes higher than the houses and hold provisions for a year. Some tribes build these storage bins inside the house, pouring the harvested grain into them through an opening in the roof.

In the plateau regions — as in some areas of Mali, Upper Volta and the Cameroun — it is difficult without a guide to reach some of the villages perched among the rocks. These still post lookouts whose duty it is to announce the stranger or enemy, whether it is some old tribal rival, the tax collector, or the vaccination team. If it is the first, the men get their weapons; if it is the second he finds no one in the village but those too old to flee.

The compounds are generally grouped in villages, com-

4

posed for the most part of members of the same clan. Among some tribes — the Lobi of Upper Volta, the Dagari and Gurunsi of Northern Ghana — a whole family occupies one vast compound surrounded by a ten or twelve foot wall with only one very narrow entrance, carefully barred at night with heavy logs. Thirty years ago, such a compound might house up to 200 or 300 persons, but now the largest shelter only 50 or 60. One of my Gurunsi friends told me that at the beginning of this century, peace and security were not the dominant features of his country. So when someone wanted to build a house outside the compound he climbed on the roof with the best archers of the village and each shot an arrow in the direction of the site chosen. Its enclosure wall was then built a certain distance beyond where the farthest arrows had fallen, and the new abode was thus considered safe from possible attack.

In the southern part of Ghana, Dahomey, and Nigeria, one finds square or rectangular houses of bamboo. These are very comfortable inside and often are furnished with taste.

In the Southern Cameroun, the suburbs of the larger towns boast wooden houses, not unlike American clapboard houses in appearance. But among the poor, the floor inside is dirt and there is little or no furniture.

Cement, brick, or prefabricated materials are becoming more and more popular among the more educated Africans, but their price is still too high for the peasants, who comprise sixty to eighty per cent of the population.

Buildings of ten to twelve stories are to be found now in the larger cities. Most are government offices but there are also some modern apartment buildings. Most Africans, however, still prefer a separate house with a little courtyard

5

or garden, to which they give a more personal touch. And among the wealthy these homes are quite luxurious.

The furniture varies with the type of habitation. The poor have a straw mat for a bed, stretched on the bare dirt floor. This is rolled up in the morning and set in a corner. Those a little better off have a bed made of reeds or a solid bench of packed clay, built out from the wall, on which they spread the traditional straw mat and whatever coverlets they have. Iron and wooden bedsteads with metal springs are now finding their way into the interior, however, and cotton mattresses, or mattresses of corn husks are appearing in the markets. Almost everywhere one finds little wooden chairs or stools, often beautifully carved or decorated with poker work.

In the poorest houses, a rope stretched from one wall to the other serves as a garment rack; again, those a little higher in the social scale keep their clothes in trunks, or in cupboards made of handsome tropical woods. In the interior, cooking utensils are still made of pottery and gourds or calabashes serve as bowls and dishes, but in the towns, enamel, aluminum, and cast ironware as well as china dishes are in common use.

The swift changes that have been taking place in tropical Africa since the end of World War II are most apparent in the cities, especially the harbor towns (Dakar, Abidjan, Lagos, Douala), whose population has increased considerably in the past ten years. This fact poses new social problems; for the newcomers are young people for the most part, drawn by the inevitable lure of the city and what seems the easy life led by their more educated fellows. They leave the tribal village and come seeking work with good pay, but often they have had no particular vocational training or may not even have finished elementary school. As a result they get only poorly paid jobs at unskilled labor and lead a miserable existence much worse from every point of view than the life they had in the village.

Village life has also modernized somewhat, but it has kept its traditional characteristics. The African woman in the village, unless she has become Christian, lives very much the same kind of life as her ancestors. Let us spend a day with one of them, who is an old friend. Her name is Kaouri and she lives in Northern Ghana.

When she comes out of her house in the morning, the sun is not yet risen. "The earth is opening," the Gurunsi say. Kaouri is going to the ceremony which will end her mother's period of mourning for her husband, who died eight months before. This is taking place ten miles away, and she has to hurry to catch the bus that leaves from Navrongo and will save her a seven mile hike. Her breakfast is a handful of peanuts and a little boiled millet left over from last night's supper, which she does not stop to reheat. Then she bends double to re-enter her house, the door of which is very low, and picks up her youngest child, a chubby boy baby six months old, who has not been given a name yet and so is called *Diampana* — "he who has no name." He does not waken as she sets him on her back and secures him with a pale blue cover cloth.

"Kaouri, are you ready?" comes a voice from outside. It belongs to Veronica, who is married to the younger brother of Kaouri's husband and who has come to get her. Veronica is going to the market in Navrongo. The two set out single file along the narrow path that circles the houses and fields.

Kaouri is twenty-three years old, sturdy, of medium

7

height and with strong features. She has a ready smile and sunny nature. She is wearing a blue cotton cloth of printed design — the latter being a picture of Kwame Nkrumah set in a garland of flowers. It is her "going out" cloth. Her work cloth is a plain dark blue that does not show the soil. Kaouri is the second wife of Abaghie, whom she married seven years ago. Her first child died shortly after birth, but she has a little girl four years old, Awopole, whom she has left in the care of her co-wife, Meggra, who is also her "sister," because their fathers were brothers.

Abaghie, who is over 40, had married Meggra fifteen years before he took Kaouri as his second wife. For Meggra he gave a bride price of two cows, five sheep, and ten pick-axes. To Meggra's mother he presented the customary gifts of tobacco, salt, and guinea hens. Meggra was a good girl who had been beautifully trained. She was tall and thin with delicate features; she was gentle, polite, submissive, and skilled at all the household tasks. She would have been perfectly happy with Abaghie if they had had a separate house. But Meggra lived with her mother-in-law, Kwora, a tall, bony domineering woman who demanded constant obedience and a great deal of work. Meggra also had to obey Kabuga, the wife of Naoua, her husband's older brother. Soon Kabuga, who was a poor cook at best and who had lost two babies, became jealous of Meggra because she was pregnant. Abaghie noticed this and did not wait for his child's birth to build the three rooms which were Meggra's right. All his relatives came to help him and a month later Meggra was installed in her own quarters, but still within the family compound.

Often, however, Meggra was very tired. She could not bring herself to ask her mother-in-law for help — much less

8

Kabuga. One day Abaghie finally said to her: "Why do you not fetch a girl from your family to help you?"

This was good advice, Meggra thought, and off she went to her father's compound. There her father chose her little sister Kaouri (the child of her father's brother) to take with her. Kaouri was then a bright and amiable nine-year-old already good at all the housekeeping chores. From that time on, the two sisters lived together, and when Kaouri was sixteen she too became the wife of Abaghie. There was no dowry to pay for her, because she was the "sister" of his first wife. But from time to time he brought gifts of millet flour, salt or tobacco to her parents and he helped them till their fields.

Meggra had had the great sorrow of watching her first baby die, despite all the remedies prescribed by the diviner and the chickens killed in honor of the ancestors.

After that her other children were brought to our Mission Medical Center (two miles away) for the slightest ache, and we took care of Meggra through all her pregnancies. She now has two boys and two girls. The eldest boy, Apuri, is eleven and Kwoto, the younger is four. Apuri is the name usually given to the first child born after the death of an infant brother. Kwoto means "he who has no father," for he was born just after his grandfather had died, and so Abaghie, as he held his infant for the first time, said: "I have no father to give you. . . ."

The elder of Meggra's little girls is eight, named Katyana, because she was born the first day of the new moon. The baby is a year old and has no name yet, but she will probably be called Kawia, for she was born during the daytime.

Apuri attends the Mission school but Abaghie has decided that his daughters will not go to school. What good

9

will it do them? If they are good housekeepers like their mother, that is enough. Besides, they say that girls who have been to school do not obey as well as the others when their father gives them a husband. . . .

As a matter of fact, the family had proof of this when Abaghie's younger brother Theophile married Veronica. She persuaded him to build their house outside the family compound, because she did not want to live with Kwora, her mother-in-law. And Kwora keeps reminding Abaghie of this "disobedience" so that he won't give in to Theophile's insistence that he send his little girls to school.

Meggra's days are very similar one to the other. When she rises in the morning she rolls up the mat that has served part mattress and part coverlet for her and her little girls. Then she goes into the courtyard and prepares a millet porridge and peanuts for the children. She sends Apuri off to school and then goes to draw water. This is an easy task since the government installed standpipes with spigots in the main centers. Before that, Meggra had to go to the small riverbed a mile and a half away, and at that time of the year there was often little water, so that she had to take her turn in the long line of women waiting to fill their jars. Now she has to walk only half a mile and turn the spigot. Home again, she sweeps out her rooms and courtyard with a broom fashioned of twigs, and then bathes the youngest children.

Abaghie is an excellent farmer. There is a majesty about him whether he is at work in the fields, clad only in a loin cloth with a goatskin slung from his shoulders to protect his back from the sun and rain, or whether his tall muscular frame is draped in the vari-colored cloth he wears on holidays in the fashion of his ancestors. Today he has been in the fields since early morning, for this is the end of May. For the past month he has been clearing the fields and burning away the bush and twigs. Their ashes make good fertilizer. It has rained now for two weeks, and the earth is moist enough to sow the early millet. Ordinarily, both wives help him. Meggra has left Katyana to take care of Kwoto and Kaouri's little girl, Awopole. She settles the baby in the cover cloth on her back, takes her hoe, hangs a gourd filled with seed from her left wrist and goes to join her husband. The two now work side by side. They scoop a little hole in the earth with the hoe and let a few seeds fall into it. The process is a study in economy of motion. A quick scooping movement with the hoe in the right hand, a toss of seeds from the left, and the hole covered over with a swish of the foot or the hoe.

Toward eleven o'clock they return home. The sun by now is high and the heat intense. Abaghie rests while Meggra feeds the children and gives her husband a little cold lunch left over from the meal of the evening before.

Toward three o'clock, the sun is less hot and Abaghie goes back to the field, this time alone, while Meggra prepares the evening meal. She shells the groundnuts for the stew, and then begins to pound the millet with a long bat-shaped pestle. This is done in a large wooden mortar which, with its pedestal, has been fashioned in one piece from a tree trunk. She lifts the pestle with both hands and brings it down in the mortar with a steady rhythmic beat. Katyana starts to help with the small pestle made especially for her, but her rhythm is a little unsteady.

"Do you need help, Meggra?" comes a voice from beyond the wall. It is Veronica, stopping by on her way home from the market because Kaouri is away. Without waiting for an

11

answer, she takes up another pestle and joins Meggra at the mortar. The thump of their pestles alternates, first one and then the other, in a perfectly synchronized and catchy beat that gets faster as they work but whose rhythm, accompanied by their soft conversation, never varies or falters.

"I would have come earlier, but I had to go to the bush for wood," Veronica explains. For her own stew she had bought dried fish and vegetables in the market. She also bought soap, she announces.

"Soap?" says Meggra with some surprise. "Don't you make it any more?"

"Oh yes, I make some. But I like bought soap for the children. It is much softer."

"Show me some?"

"I'll bring you some tomorrow."

Meggra has always admired Veronica, first because from the day of her wedding she has succeeded in escaping the authority of her mother-in-law, and then because she is "modern" and not at all timid about trying the new things that come from the outside.

It isn't necessary to bend double to enter her house, because the doors are as tall as a person; and then she has lanterns, with which one can go out at night even when there is no moon. She has a pressure lamp in her house, too, that makes almost as much light as daytime. It was very expensive and Veronica had to make and sell soap for three months to have enough money to buy it. Meggra would be glad to do the same to have such a lamp instead of the little bowl of vegetable oil with an old strip of rag for a wick. But it is best not to think about it. Kwora would be angry and Kabuga too jealous. Veronica does not have this trouble because she lives with her husband and children outside the family compound, and so is not exposed to their unkind remarks. And then, she has been to domestic science school, and knows how to do a number of clever things. Meggra sighs to herself at times, wishing she could be like Veronica. She is very fond of her besides, for Veronica is always ready to help or do a kindness without waiting to be asked and without expecting some service in return.

"What else can I do?" asks Veronica as they finish pounding.

"Nothing else, thank you. I can do the rest myself."

"Well, I must run to get my supper. But I'll come tomorrow."

"Many thanks, Veronica. And God be with you."

Meggra now sets about sifting the pounded millet. After sifting it, she takes it into the house to grind it. Fitted into an earthen stand built against the wall are two flat granite-like stones. This is the typical hand mill of the savanna people. Meggra places a small handful of the pounded millet on one of the stones and grinds down on it in a quick sliding motion with another flat stone held in both hands. These stones are soon worn smooth and it becomes necessary to roughen them by hitting them with a hard sharpened pebble. That is why there are two stones in the stand although only one is in use at a time.

To grind enough millet flour for the evening meal takes over an hour. Then comes the long cooking, while the bubbling millet is stirred constantly to keep it from getting lumpy. When it is the right consistency — about that of thick cornmeal mush — so that it can be easily picked up in the fingers, Meggra divides it into two enamel bowls. Then she tests the stew that has been simmering over another small fire. It is a thick stew of crushed groundnuts, red pepper, shea butter, daw-saw seeds, and dried fish. This she also divides into two bowls. One bowl of millet and another of stew are shared by Abaghie and his eldest son Apuri. They take a piece of cooked millet in their fingers and dip it into the stew. It thus takes the place both of bread and spoon. Meggra takes her meal with the girls and little Kwoto, who is being taught his manners. When he is older, he will eat with his father and brother.

After supper, Abaghie can generally be found chatting with his brothers. Meggra puts the leftovers away, washes the bowls with a vegetable sponge, folds her children in the straw mat that serves as both bed and blanket, and then sits in her small courtyard, shelling groundnuts by moonlight until Abaghie comes home and calls her for the night.

Ten miles away, Kaouri is taking part in the ceremony that ends the period of mourning for her father. He had been called Teddam, master of strength. The village smith — who is also master of ritual — shaves the head of Adiounta, Kaouri's mother. She was Teddam's first wife, the We Kane, or wife given by God. The ceremony is not necessary for his other widows. Nearby, a concoction of leaves is simmering over the fire, and this will be used to shampoo Adiounta. To make sure that it will have the necessary virtue to loose her from all bonds to her dead husband, a libation of flour water is first poured over the pot in which it is heating.

When the ceremony is over, everyone rejoices, the dances begin, and the festivities last far into the night. The next morning Kaouri goes back to her husband's home and the daily routine begins again.

She and Meggra each have small plots of land, on which they grow groundnuts, tomatoes, sorrel, peppers, onions, and herbs for the usual stew. These fields they take care of themselves besides helping Abaghie with the weeding and hoeing of the family fields. Periodically they must also resurface the dirt floor of their quarters and courtyard with a fresh layer of mud. This they pack down with a crude wooden tool shaped more or less like a foot. Then comes the harvest time, and finally the dry season. This is when the women brew the millet beer, make the shea butter, and if all goes well, they have time to fashion the pretty pieces of pottery that adorn their house. This is the time, too, to resurface the walls of the compound, which they paint with a thick liquid made from the pods of the néré tree.[1] The walls are then rubbed down for hours with a hard stone until they are smooth. This is the way of life, more or less of rural women in Northern Ghana, and it is similar to that of all women of the savanna with a few local variations. In regions where cloth garments have been in use since time immemorial, the wife cultivates a field of cotton, the product of which she spins during the dry season.

Obviously, Africa's rural women are always busy. Just the preparation of the day's main meal takes hours. Yet many of them are now taking an active interest in community activities to improve their villages. When they are like Veronica, gentle and amiable, they form a link between the old and new, persuading mothers to send their little girls to school, explaining why some old customs that were good for their grandfathers are not accepted by their children. They are the natural leaders, for they know their traditions and they are sensitive to how much can be changed without causing conflict in their society.

---

[1] The néré (Parkia Biglobesa) is a tree found throughout the West African savanna. The black kernels contained in the pods are cooked and fermented, and then used in stews.

15

Life in a Muslim family varies somewhat. I well remember an enjoyable visit with Moussa, who lives in one of the larger towns of the Mali Republic.

Moussa is a notable, a member of the great Keita family. He was born in Kangaba, between Bamako and Siguiri, in the ancestral home of the Keita, filled with mementos of the illustrious members of the family. Among them are souvenirs of Soundiata Keita, who ruled over the Mandingo empire in the thirteenth century and introduced the culture and weaving of cotton, and of Gingo-Moussa, who at the beginning of the fourteenth century, introduced the construction of square houses with flat roofs and brought the Mandingo empire to the peak of its power.

At the beginning of World War II Moussa enlisted as a rifleman, was wounded and subsequently hospitalized in France. After the armistice he returned home and a short time later was appointed chief of police in one of the larger cities.

During the war his two wives had been left in his mother's care. Upon his return he married another young wife, permitted him by Muslim law, so that he might have many children.

Moussa owns his own house and land. The living quarters are arranged around a huge courtyard. They are built of sun-dried bricks like all the other houses in the town, but instead of the usual clay roof, Moussa's are roofed with corrugated iron sheeting. This doubles the life of the walls since it keeps the rainwater from seeping into them.

One of Moussa's daughters had just graduated with honors from our Mission primary school while I was on a visit there. He had been so pleased with her success that he had sent the Sisters a huge plate of *tô* — the specialty of

16

the region — and I was more than happy to accompany our headmistress on her "thank you" visit. Moussa would be glad, I was told, to answer my questions on family life.

Moussa introduced us to his mother, Korotoumou, and we greeted her in the Bambara language. Her welcome was warmly cordial, and she invited us to visit the quarters.

Each of Moussa's wives has two rooms for herself. In one of these there is a metal bedstead with a straw mattress, coverlets, and a mosquito netting. At one end of the room stand two or three large baskets filled with cotton. There are colorful garments hanging at the other end, and here and there on the floor a straw mat that takes the place of a chair. The second is a kind of storeroom in which supplies of rice, millet, and cotton are kept, together with chests of clothing. Each set of rooms has a small porch facing the courtyard and separated from the next by a partition.

Korotoumou's quarters are like the others, but contain more chests and trunks, for in addition to her own clothing she keeps her son's suits and uniforms and the cloth and garments he is setting aside to give to his wives and children. Her bed had no netting. Moussa told us he had given her one, but she wasn't used to it so she kept it carefully folded in one of the chests.

Moussa hospitably took us through his private rooms too. Their white-washed walls emphasized their meticulous neatness. His sitting room contained a large sofa bed — very good for naps, he observed smilingly — a table on which stood several photographs and a handsome coffee service, and a long set of shelves filled with books, newspapers, and souvenirs brought from Paris; among the latter were two alarm clocks. The door to his bedroom stood ajar revealing a huge bed; visible through the netting was a magnificent

17

coverlet woven in the lovely blue and white checked pattern traditional in that part of the country.

When we came out into the courtyard again, the woman had returned to their daily chores. Moussa's two younger wives, seated on straw mats in the shade, were busy with the cotton, one combing it with a large metal comb, and the other spinning. Moussa's first wife, with the help of the daughter of one of her co-wives, had begun to pound the millet. Korotoumou was salting big chunks of fish before dropping them in the thick spicy tomato sauce bubbling in a huge iron pot set on stones over a wood fire. It was the usual supper stew but it seemed to have a special fragrance that afternoon and Korotoumou was pleased to be asked what spices she preferred. The noon meal is usually rice, she told us, which does not take so long to prepare.

Moussa had chairs brought into the court for us and with a gracious gesture invited my questions. He looked very grand and almost fatherly in the wide Bambara tunic or *boubou* that he had exchanged for his policeman's uniform.

"My mother is the real mistress of the house," he began. "She directs my wives and me too. Thanks to her, everything goes along swimmingly, and we never have any annoyances or disagreements. In the morning I ask her what we are going to have for dinner. She tells me, and I say, 'That's fine' — even if I don't particularly care for it." He then turned to Korotoumou and asked her to tell us an anecdote from the family history. Her answer was one of diplomatic simplicity: "You are too young to speak of these things." What she really meant was that the subject was not one to discuss with strangers.

"Do all families where there is more than one wife always get along this well?" I asked.

"There are families like mine, where everyone gets along very well. There are others where there is bickering and quarreling every day, because there is no one exercising enough authority."

"In fact, your mother runs your house," I said. "But when the husband's mother is no longer alive, does each wife do as she pleases?"

"Most often it is the first wife who takes over, but if she is not very responsible or capable, the husband chooses another as the mistress of the house and he tells the others they must obey her."

"Who is responsible for the meals when there is more than one wife?" I asked.

"I buy the millet and rice, and each morning I give the wife in charge of the cooking money to buy meat and "ingredients" — that is, spices. Each wife takes a two-day turn at cooking, beginning with the evening meal, and during that time she sleeps with me."

"Do you all take your meals together?"

"I eat with my eldest boys and the sons of my friends who are living here with me while they go to school. My three wives take their meals together, and my mother eats with my daughters and the little boys so that she can teach them good manners."

At this point a friend of Moussa's, a civil servant named Youssouf, cycled into the courtyard. He belonged to the malaria control squad and was on his periodic inspection tour. It was his business to make sure no stagnant water was collecting anywhere. Moussa explained my interest in family life. The conversation turned on the way marriages are arranged, and I asked whether it would not be better if the young women could choose for themselves. Both became very grave. Girls should obey their fathers in this matter, they felt. But fathers are wrong to force their daughters against their will or choose husbands who are not good providers.

Moussa, who as a police officer, must often investigate the charges brought to him, was more ready to concede that a father's wrong choice could be a serious thing. He had had a case a few days before of a young woman whose older husband (about sixty) gave her only 15 cents a day, not enough even for the stew.

"When I asked her why she had accepted this man for her husband," Moussa said that she replied, 'How could I say no to my father!' "

Even if the husband is a good provider, however, he must be careful not to play favorites. He must treat all his wives equally as the custom demands.

"You must give all of them the same thing on the same day," Moussa continued. "For instance, if I buy cloths for my wives, they must all be the same."

"And do you buy three at once?"

"When I don't have enough money for all three, I buy them one at a time, but I save them up until I have three. Then I give them to my mother who distributes them."

"You are a good husband," Youssouf intervened. "Your wives are all very happy with you."

"I try to please them," Moussa answered earnestly. "I give each of them money to buy cotton. That cotton belongs to them. They can spin it, dye it, and weave it to suit themselves. . . ."

"My first wife runs my house," Youssouf offered. "The other two obey her, but sometimes I have to intervene if she has been too bossy. We older men — I am 55 — have

20

been married a long time; but the young men now take only one wife. Then there is no trouble, and the family gets along better."

"Perhaps that is true," said Moussa. "In any case our children will be happier than we. They are going to school and things will be better for them."

I have since noted that the well-educated generally have only one wife. I have known others, however, both Muslim and animist, who find polygamy to their advantage and justify it now on the ground that it is *African*.

"We get better service this way," they will tell you laughingly. "When we have more than one wife, they compete for our favor."

But educated African women are generally opposed to polygamy.

What of Christian families? In rural areas, husband and wife work together in the fields, and their daily lives in general are similar to Abaghie's and Meggra's, except that the marriage is monogamous.

In towns it varies, especially in the more prosperous regions. Ilesha, for example, is a city of about 80,000 inhabitants in the Yoruba, or southwestern, province of Nigeria. This is the average size of towns in Yoruba country, the capital of which, Ibadan, has a population of 500,000.

Ilesha's houses increasingly are being built of brick or cement, with corrugated metal roofs that gleam white in the sunshine. Most families of modest means live in houses built of sun-baked clay (which is very solid once it has hardened) covered with cement inside and out both to strengthen the walls and to improve their appearance.

It is in one of these houses that my friend Louisa lives.

21

Her husband is headmaster in the Mission school and has fourteen teachers under him.

Louisa was born in Ife in 1919, in one of the vast family compounds, also built of mudbrick. Her father Charles, a mason, occupied three rooms in the compound with Juliana and their children. The furniture was the old type: straw mats for beds, wooden chests for the best clothes, and everyday garments hung on a cord stretched between two beams.

Charles's eldest brother Baba Ifa was a diviner. He possessed a *Fâ* (divinity) that people came to consult in order to have children, to cure a sickness, and many other things. In the great hall of the compound, which could hold about 100 persons, there was a small platform, on which the sunlight shone through a barred window that looked out on the courtyard. On the platform rested a jar covered with a beautiful hand-woven cloth and topped by a richly fashioned pearl tiara; inside was the *Fâ*. To consult the *Fâ*, Baba Ifa performed the prescribed rite with a carved wooden tray and a delicately sculptured ivory horn. He then told his client what to do — i.e., what animal to bring for the sacrifice (a chicken, goat, or sheep) — or he dispensed the proper remedy for the illness, or the belt guaranteed to insure pregnancy. For the more important ceremonies, a large crowd gathered in the great room and Baba Ifa, dressed in a magnificent robe of red velvet embroidered with gold braid, presided over the ritual, consisting of prayers, dances, and chants.

Charles, however, had become a Christian and married a young Christian girl, Juliana. Of their five children, two had died in infancy. Their son Pascal was twelve years old, and their little girls Louisa and Helen, were five and two when Charles was killed in an accident. This was in 1924. He was supervising the building of a new town hall when he fell from the scaffolding and died shortly afterward of a fractured skull.

Juliana was inconsolable and refused to remarry. She continued as before to trade for a living. Baba Ifa assumed the expenses for Pascal's schooling and he later entered government service. The girls came to the Mission school, but Louisa preferred going to market with her mother, and when she was twelve years old she left school altogether. From then on her time was divided between keeping house and going to market with Juliana. When she was eighteen, in 1937, she married Joseph and came with him to live in Ilesha. She, too, lost two babies in infancy, but raised five. The eldest — Junice, born in 1940 — was called Aramide, which indicated that an elder sister had died. The name literally means "my body has come back" and suggests an old Yoruba belief in the transmigration of souls. Junice has just finished nurses' training and has gone for further study at the hospital in Lagos. She is engaged to be married soon to a young doctor. Louisa's son Raphael, born in 1943, is studying at Ibadan University. He, too, has an African name, Baba-tunde, which means "my father has come back." In other words, as the eldest son, he will take his father's place and, it is hoped, support the family. The three youngest, Agnes, Cecilia, and Lucien, go to the Mission school.

Louisa, a large, vigorous woman in her prime, with a pleasant face and an air of elegance in her Yoruba blue dress, is a hard worker, intent upon ensuring a good education for her children. On a typical day she is up at dawn. Very often she walks to early Mass with her neighbor, while her husband bicycles to Church. Home again, she gives the

23

children their breakfast — usually cornmeal mush — and sends them off to school. Then she rolls up the mosquito netting, makes the beds, sweeps the rooms, dusts the furniture, which is modern, and gives a whisk of the cloth over the holy pictures and family photos that crowd one wall of the living room and spill over on the two end tables. Then, on the table, she sets green beans and cornmeal mush left over from supper and covers them with a napkin, ready for her family when they come home for lunch.

She next rolls up a little of the cornmeal mush to take with her. From under her bed she pulls a large white enamel pan filled with cloths of every color, remnants and underclothes. This she sets on her head and is off to the market where she will stay until evening. Louisa has a regular place because she pays for a license and she does a brisk business. Each month she buys about $200 worth of cloth and $100 in other merchandise, including headkerchiefs and undergarments. Sometimes a dealer who has just received a new shipment of brand new prints will offer her the lot if she will also buy $10 worth of soap or sugar. She usually accepts, since this will give her an "exclusive," and as for the sugar or soap, she sells it more cheaply than the shops and is rid of it in two days, content to make only a minimal profit. Her average net per month is from $18 to $20, which is no small sum in a country where teachers earn $50 per month. Her husband, who is a headmaster, earns $70. But the cost of living is not very high in Ilesha. The rent for their five rooms is $12 a month and food averages $8 a month per person. Every Friday evening the whole family goes to the cocoa farm where they work all day Saturday, returning late in the evening. The cocoa earns Junice's tuition at nurses' training school in Lagos.

24

"Wouldn't you rather stay at home?" I asked Louisa one hot January Sunday when she mentioned being tired after her week in the market. I had gone to spend the afternoon with her at her request. The children were at the school games and her husband was at a meeting. She gave a surprised little laugh at my question. She could not stay home even if she wanted to she said; the market was in her blood. Besides, it was much more interesting than staying home, what with all the people she saw and the news she heard. And then, she added, becoming serious, what she earned paid her daughter's board and room in Lagos, which is more expensive than Ilesha. Junice needed 15 dollars a month for food and 5 dollars for her room. Her mother sent her $10 a month pocket money besides, and with the rest of her earnings paid the family food bill. Her husband Joseph paid their son's tuition.

Didn't she feel the younger children were being neglected? I asked her. She thought not. Before leaving in the morning she prepared their lunch, which they ate with their father. She had a young girl servant who joined her in the market in the early afternoon and tended the stall while she herself bought provisions for the evening meal. The girl took them home, began the cooking and set the table. When Louisa got home she had only to give the meal the finishing touches. The family had dinner together. The maid washed the dishes and then left, taking with her enough supper for her mother and little brother. In addition, Louisa paid her $12 a month, which was generous, since a house boy who stayed all day received an average wage of $20 a month. The food Louisa donated, she said, because the girl's mother was very poor. Her husband had deserted her, and for a while she had managed to get along selling fruit. One day, however, a motorcyclist had knocked her into the path of an oncoming truck, and both her legs had been broken. She had spent two months in the hospital, but still found it difficult to walk.

"Don't you see, Sister, why we African women have to know how to earn our own living?" It was the same explanation I had heard so many times. "We never know what will happen — and a woman is hard put to it if her husband does not give her enough to feed and educate the children. I am lucky; Joseph is a wonderful husband. But look at my sister."

This was a surprise to me, for Helen seemed to have made a good match. According to Louisa, however, her husband Daniel was too rich for their own good. He had not wanted Helen to work or trade, and since she loved him very much she had agreed. Then one day he brought a second wife home. She was the woman who cooked his food when he was on an inspection tour of his cocoa plantations, and she had borne his child. At first, he had visited her regularly at her parents' home, but soon after the child was born her parents had demanded that Daniel marry her. Helen's first impulse had been to leave, but she had no means of her own and could not earn enough to keep herself and her two little girls. Daniel begged her to remain; he had allowed himself to be persuaded to take a second wife, but he wasn't very happy about it. Helen gave in and stayed. She was still in love with him, and she hoped that somehow the matter could be straightened out.

Had Daniel given up being a Christian? I asked Louisa.

"No," she answered. "He still is faithful to the Mission. He is really very uneasy about the whole situation but he does not have the courage to send away the second wife."

Cocoa was then selling at a high price Louisa said, so

Daniel was able to pay the bride dowry demanded by the second wife's father, build a large new brick house at a cost of $10,000 and keep his sons in boarding school in England.

I expressed my sympathy for Helen.

"Oh she is quite lucky at that," said Louisa. "At least Daniel gives her money. There are so many like her who have to support themselves and their children because their husbands give them nothing. . . . That is why I said that we all have to have our own means of support." What she said was true of almost all Yoruba women. Those her age are almost all traders, a few own trucks, and most of them earn a tidy sum. One trader of Louisa's acquaintance made a profit of about $300 a month, she said, although she was something of an exception.

Many women are dressmakers and their earnings range from thirty to 100 dollars a month. Salesgirls and other shop clerks receive a salary of from $25 to $40, nurses and teachers $50 to $70 and civil servants from $150 to $300 depending on their category, competence, and length of service.

Now more and more children are going to school, especially in the towns. In rural areas about half attend primary school, but a great effort is being made to extend at least primary education to all children. There is no school fee, and all pupils receive free medical care. Ilesha's people are progressive. They have good roads, running water, and electricity. But to have progress, Louisa observed, you must pay for it. "That is why our taxes are rather high and it costs more to live here."

While we were chatting it grew dark; the heat of the day was retreating before a brisk little breeze.

As she turned on the lamps, Louisa came to the point

27

of Helen's story. Could we not take her girls at the Sister's boarding school in Oshogbo? She and Helen and their mother Juliana had all gone to school with the Sisters, she reminded us. We promised to write the Superior at Oshogbo that evening, and shortly afterward took our leave.

"Thank you, Sister, and God go with you," she called after us.

"And God be with you, Louisa."

On our way home, Sister Patricia, who was new to our Mission, was very thoughtful.

"There must be some way to protect a monogamous marriage from situations like Helen's."

"It will come," I said, "when women's equality and rights are recognized by law. Several of my friends in Togo, Dahomey, and elsewhere have found themselves in similar circumstances without redress. At first, the marriage seemed a stable, happy one. Then after a few years, the husband got bored, decided he needed 'a spare tire,' as he put it, and got himself a concubine in town. After a while, he brought her home — and frequently if the wife protested, she was sent away."

"What can a woman do in a case like that?" Sister Patricia asked.

"Most of them have some means of earning a living, either a job or a stand in the market. I have known some who have put aside their savings for just such a rainy day. But this does not prevent their suffering cruelly at the sudden discovery that their husbands have deceived them for some time and abused their confidence. There are women who have contributed their earnings to the purchase of a house and have then found themselves on the outside when their husbands decided to bring home a concubine or two."

"Doesn't a wife have some redress then? Is there no way to get her money back?"

"No way at all. She is on her own from then on. Louisa was right when she said African women have to have their own sources of income."

"But what if the husband earns a good salary?"

"Many of them think that what they earn belongs to them personally and is not to be used for family expenses. This is inherited from the old custom whereby it was the wife's duty to till her fields and provide the food for herself and her children. The husband supplied only the meat, and that when he went hunting.

"In the towns now, the women have no fields or gardens to cultivate, but the old mentality still persists — they are expected to support themselves and their children, while the husband feels obliged only to provide an occasional present.

"There are exceptions, of course. We both know many Africans who do support their families. More and more will do so as education is extended, and obviously Christianity has had a tremendous influence in this direction. As for the women, in all my years here I have never failed to be impressed by their courage and the delicacy and patience with which they hide their own feelings so that their children will respect their father. They deserve all the help we can give them to achieve some type of legal protection in cases like these."

2. The Burden of History

Whenever I asked one of my friends in Dahomey about the family customs in her country, she invariably answered: "That depends, Mother." And it depends on so many things — on the family situation, its social status, the environment, tradition, education, personal development, individual temperament, religious practices. . . .

If one were to ask, "Do American women work or do they remain at home? Are they concerned about the education of their children? Is divorce common? Are they religious?" — our answer too, would invariably be, "That depends."

In sub-Saharan Africa, the situation is still more complex. We must keep in mind the great diversity of peoples and their particular customs, the changes wrought by European presence, and the strength of their ancestral cultures.

Although the interior of the African continent was for a long time isolated by its natural barriers — the Sahara in the north, its difficult and dangerous coastline — it had nevertheless its own history and civilizations. Some little knowledge of them — even if sketchy — is necessary to understand its inhabitants and the way they live.

Ancient history, which has so much to say of North

Africa (Carthage, Libya, Egypt), tells us practically nothing about sub-Saharan Africa. Some scholars think that the first inhabitants, believed to be Negroes of small stature, were to be found there more than 6000 years ago. According to some historians of ancient times, Negroes were occupying about the same African territories they do today in the fifth century B.C.

We know a little more about medieval Africa, which left vestiges of great kingdoms and empires. Among the more famous was the empire of Ghana, which began its rise around the fourth century A.D. and reached its peak in the tenth century. It lay to the northeast of present-day Ghana, between Timbuktoo and the Senegal river. Envied by its ambitious neighbors, it was forced into deadly wars and its capital was sacked three times. Then the gradual spread of the desert through the whole region led to terrible famines and by the fourteenth century the empire of Ghana had ceased to exist.

But other empires were flourishing — the Songhai, with Gao as its capital, and Mali or Mandingo, which began modestly on the banks of the Niger at Kangaba at the beginning of the seventh century. Its chiefs, the Keita, established relations with the neighboring states, and gradually, by war and alliances, extended their power as far as Gao. In the fourteenth century, the Mali empire, still governed by the Keita dynasty, included almost the entire left bank of the Niger as far as Gao. The Arabian geographer, Ibn Battuta, describes it as a prosperous state because of its gold mines. He admires the courtesy and discipline of its officials, the splendor and ceremony of its royal functions, the respect and obedience given the commands of the sovereign and the decisions of the chiefs. In the seventeenth

31

century, the advent of the Bambara kingdoms of Segu and Kaarta brought about the gradual decline of the Mali Empire. In the loop of the Niger, other empires had taken shape in the eleventh century, among them the Mossi empires of Ougadougou and Yatenga, which still survive. Their structure is hierarchical, divided into provinces, cantons, and villages. Each province chief, like the emperor, has a council of ministers, dignitaries of his court, and pages. The canton and village chiefs are responsible to him. The chiefdom is hereditary, but does not pass necessarily from father to son. The emperor chooses, among the relatives of the deceased, the one he thinks most capable.

These empires had no written history. The genealogy of the chiefs, the story of the migrations and other events which affected the life of the clans, were all recorded in the memory and passed on in the oral tradition of the tribe. In the great clans, certain attendants of the chiefs were assigned to memorize their history and to recount it while singing the praises of the various chiefs.

The administrative structure and civilization of these different empires was quite complex. There were forms of courtesy that recall the old Assyrian and Egyptian empires and a hierarchical structure reminiscent of feudalism. Their artisans — working in wood, leather, metal — used techniques similar to those common in Mediterranean countries of the same period.

From the fifteenth to the seventeenth centuries there grew up other kingdoms — the Ewe in Togo; the Fanti, Ga, and Ashanti in Ghana; the Fon in Dahomey; the Yoruba and Benin in Nigeria, to mention just a few. Their populations were especially distinguished for their artistic and intellectual abilities and their talent for commerce and trade.

Africans are justly proud of these centuries of history; the record is as filled with splendid deeds of bravery and heroism and valiant exploits as the history of other peoples. There were tyrants — just as there were in Europe — but there were also wise and prudent kings who ruled their people with justice, within the framework of a political and social organization similar in many ways to that of ancient Europe.

In the forests and savannas dwelt other extremely interesting populations. They were usually excellent and hardy farmers and brave warriors, whose fiercely independent spirit kept them from forming kingdoms strong enough to resist the invasions of their powerful neighbors or to negotiate alliances with them. Down through the centuries, they were raided by stronger nations and led into slavery. A certain number remained in the country but many were sold abroad, either by the Arabs who transported them across the Sahara to the slave markets of North Africa, or by European slave traders who bought them from the chiefs of the coastal kingdoms and sold them in America. . . . Thousands and thousands of Negroes were thus snatched from their villages and transplanted to far-off lands in inhuman conditions despite the successive interdictions and excommunications of various popes — Alexander VI in the fifteenth century, Urban VIII in the seventeenth, down to the condemnations of slavery issued by Gregory XVI in 1839 and Leo XIII in 1888.

In 1807, slave trade was forbidden in British possessions and in 1831 it was suppressed in territories under French control. But it continued elsewhere. The antislavery campaign conducted in Europe by Cardinal Lavigerie, among others, led in 1890 to the Berlin Agreement, by which the

33

European powers were pledged to take effective measures against the crime of slave trading. It finally disappeared with the abolition of slavery in the Americas, but there is still sporadic slave traffic on a smaller scale in Saudi Arabia, where slavery is still recognized by law.

There is still some social distinction in Africa today between the descendants of former slaves and those of free ancestors. Chiefs and notables, however, continue to protect the descendants of former slaves of their families.

The Cameroun includes a great variety of ethnic groups, Bantu and semi-Bantu for the most part, who settled in the country comparatively recently. The Bamileke, semi-Bantu, probably came from the East and North in successive waves between the sixteenth and seventeenth centuries, taking possession of the fertile plateaus in the West. Their chiefdoms have remained independent instead of grouping together into kingdoms. The length of a dynasty is counted by the number of chiefs' skulls it has kept. (There are chiefdoms of eleven skulls, seventeen skulls, etc.) The Bamoun, who came later, defeated the Bamileke and settled in the region of Foumban. At the end of the eighteenth century, the Foulbe, a shepherd people of Hamitic origin, arrived from Nigeria after a long period of migration and thanks to their cavalry succeeded in pushing back up into the mountains the indigenous inhabitants of the Northern Cameroun, usually called Kirdi.

The southern region, inhabited by Negroes, underwent the successive but more or less peaceful invasion of Bantu, Bete, Bassa, Bakoko, and finally Douala, who took over the coastal area during the seventeenth century. The other populations (Bulu, Ewondo, Eton, etc.), who were still migrating when European penetration began, settled in the central part of the country.

Among the Camerounians, it appears that only the Bassa and Douala trafficked in slaves.

European colonization began in the nineteenth century, bringing with it both the well-known benefits and abuses.

The missionaries, however, had come before the colonial powers. Wherever they could, they opened schools and dispensaries, made friends with the chiefs, and in general respected the customs of the various peoples. This respect was for Catholic missionaries a specific directive of the Sacred Congregation for the Propagation of the Faith.

The Africans are naturally proud of their ancestral cultures, which possessed the basic values of all civilizations worthy of the name: a respect for sacred things, respect for authority, family unity, sound training of the children, respect for work, and the practice of mutual aid.

This ancient civilization is being rapidly modified by new influences — different ways of thinking, living, dressing, working — and sub-Saharan Africa is leaping over in a few decades the stages of development Europe took centuries to traverse. In 20 or 30 years, the African interior has gone from portage to air transport, from illiteracy to university studies, from the most autocratic feudal systems to universal suffrage. In every family today there is a marked difference between the elders and the young people, and as in every transitional period, traditional customs exist side by side with new usages.

"We are seven centuries behind Europe," a Mali notable once said to me. And it is easy to understand how the great gap between the old and the new sometimes leads to tragic misunderstandings. Clan elders, used to complete

35

authority and unquestioning obedience, find it difficult to sympathize with the new aspirations of their grandchildren and think them merely rebellious. The youngsters, on the other hand, feel their personal hopes and wishes belittled, their dawning individuality stifled by the absolute authoritarianism of their chiefs, and find it hard to submit to decisions they consider arbitrary.

But changes are occurring rapidly. Customs that still prevail in a rural area are hardly observed in towns. A problem that is acute in one region, no longer exists four or five hundred miles away. In many places — and among many families — the fusion of moral and cultural riches of other peoples with the authentic traditional values of African culture takes place very naturally. And often the old and new exist side by side in curious harmony, as the following examples will show.

My young friend Aminata had just had her first baby, and she was very proud of the truly fine layette she had prepared for it. This violated the custom, which considered it bad luck for the newborn child, but she had no worries. Aminata was one of our former students and so we were among her first visitors. Her room was full of friends, both European and African. The former had sent flowers or candy and their gifts were pretty embroidered bibs and baby clothes. African friends had brought the customary gifts: baskets of fine white millet, the basic food of the country, or choice cotton ready for spinning; the "ingredients" recommended for young mothers; a necklace of aromatic roots so that the odor of milk would not bother her; and the *dyala* or orange ribbon with which young mothers bind their foreheads for three months if the child is a boy and four if it is a girl. Some of her younger friends had come with

36

sweaters or embroidered garments they had made themselves.

There were congratulations for Aminata and admiration for her baby boy, with his pale skin and black curly hair, sleeping with little fists closed tight.

"What a beautiful baby!" the Europeans cooed. "How nice and chubby he is! What pretty dimples!"

"What an ugly little thing he is," the African women exclaimed. "Such a homely face!" According to ancestral belief, to praise a newborn infant is to attract the attention of evil spirits, who are always prowling about everywhere and who might hurt him out of envy. But then the traditional wish is always added, too: "May God grant that he live! May God grant him health, happiness, and many little brothers."

Aminata asked us to stay a while after the others had gone. She was radiantly happy. Yosefou, her husband, was doubly so because he had wanted a boy so much. "See, Sister, the beautiful pendant he gave me!" Aminata said. It was a lovely gold filigree locket.

"Are your parents coming to see you?" we asked.

"I think so. Yosefou telephoned his mother and father and wired mine. But," she added smiling, "you know that I have an old aunt, my grandmother's sister, who thinks we neglected our customs too much when we married, so we have decided to inform her in the old way. One of Yosefou's friends has gone to toss a rooster into her yard."

"You throw a hen if it is a girl, I think."

"Yes, Sister . . . but don't you think the telephone is a little more practical?"

"Yes, but in olden days, there were no telephones, and the custom had its meaning and symbolism. What will you name your baby?"

37

"I don't know; my husband's father hasn't decided yet. You know that as head of the family he must name the baby seven days after birth in the presence of the whole family gathering. We think his name will be Mamadou; in any case, that will be his second name if my father-in-law gives him another."

"Will you have any of the customary ceremonies?"

"No, we'll just call in the marabout and shave the baby's head . . . but we are going to have a reception for all our friends. I hope you will come, Sisters."

"If we are free, we shall be glad to come, Aminata. God keep you, and may He make your little boy strong and healthy and give you other children."

"Amina," she said, as we took our leave. The word means "may all your wishes come true."

"May all these presents bring you luck," we answered.

"Amina," she said again. "My greetings to all the Sisters."

I remember when Arthur, the son of one very good African friend, took suddenly ill. There had been a big dinner to celebrate his graduation. Afterward he and some friends went for a long bicycle ride under the broiling sun and then took a dip in the river. He came home with a fever and so did two of his companions. The doctor diagnosed the trouble as food poisoning complicated by amoebic dysentery. But Noara, Arthur's old grandmother, was convinced he had been poisoned by a jealous schoolmate. He had never been sick before.

It was useless to tell her Arthur had no enemies, that all the dinner guests were his friends and above suspicion.

"Do we ever know when we have enemies?" Noara insisted. "Besides, a friend can be an intermediary without knowing it and have you drink the poison while he thinks he is giving you something that's good for you." To put her own heart at rest she returned to her village, without telling anyone, to consult the diviner.

I had known Noara for many years, and I had known her mother and father, who was a great chief. She had been quite lovely as a girl, and some of that youthful beauty still lingered in her delicate features, the proud tilt of her head and the dignity of her bearing. She was one of my good friends, the favorite wife of a canton chief, the one he trusted implicitly. It was she who took care of his robes and prepared his food because he was afraid of being poisoned by his other wives. They were jealous of his beautiful new bride of sixteen and had been sulky with the head wife.

Noara was now sixty years old, but her anxiety for Arthur quickened her firm, even stride, and she walked the ten miles to her village apparently unwearied. What happened next I knew from having witnessed it another time, and we may imagine we are with her. First she prostrated herself before her husband after the fashion of Mossi women.

"Arthur is sick," she announced.

Naba (chief) Kobré was seated in his courtyard, deeply absorbed in a magazine. Four page boys sat squatted on mats around him, ready to do his bidding at the slightest sign. Contrary to Noara's expectation, he was unimpressed by the news she brought.

"I know. Our son Pierre telephoned me."

"I'm afraid he's been poisoned."

"Do you think so?" Naba Kobré became serious immediately.

"Yes. I do believe so."

A page was dispatched for a chicken and five minutes

later Noara was on her way to the diviner in the chief's auto. Sitting beside her was the page boy holding a live chicken.

After the customary greetings, Noara began: "I bring you this chicken because Arthur, my grandson, is sick. The doctors have been taking care of him for three days but he is no better. Has he not been poisoned?"

"I shall see," the soothsayer answered calmly.

He took up a handful of white shells as he asked, "How has such a thing happened to this healthy boy?"

"He went to bathe near the *tangande*[1] of Kougi," said Noara, "and on his way home the fever seized him."

The diviner then threw the shells on the ground and carefully examined the way they fell. After two or three anxious minutes he declared: "Arthur has not been poisoned, but he leaned his bicycle against the *tangande* before he bathed. Then he broke off a branch of the sacred tree to fan himself. He lay down in the shade of the sacred tree and fell asleep. During this time, his soul went out of his body, and the spirit of the *tangande* took it and kept it prisoner."[2]

"Can you free it?" asked Noara anxiously.

"Follow me into my courtyard and I shall ask the spirit of my *tangande* to deliver it."

The diviner squatted in front of the stone on which sacrifices are offered. He first cut the chicken's throat and let the blood run on the stone. Then he let go of the hen, which toppled over on its back. A broad smile lit up his face for this meant the sacrifice was accepted. He next plucked out

---

[1] A sacred thicket which, the pagans believe, is inhabited by spirits.

[2] Pagan Africans think that the soul leaves the body during sleep and goes for a walk. It is then very vulnerable and can be wounded or taken prisoner, or even eaten by an enemy.

a few feathers and stuck them on the blood. Then he pushed the hen's beak against the ground, saying, "May the genie of the *tangande* invert thus the head of the enemies." He stood the hen upright and intoned: "May the friends remain upright."

Next he broke one of the hen's claws saying, "I break the feet of the male enemy." He broke the other claw saying, "I break the feet of the female enemy."

All this time, Noara crouched beside the diviner, holding a calabash half-filled with water and praying to the spirit of the *tangande* to give back the soul of her grandson. When the hen fell over it meant that the spirit had gone to deliver the captive soul and would return and place it in the water of the calabash. When the sacrifice was ended, the sooth-sayer whistled softly, as if to call someone; then he made a sign to Noara who quickly slipped the lid over the cala-bash, into which she believed Arthur's soul had just been returned. She rewarded the diviner generously and thanked him profusely. Then she hurried back to town. She managed to enter Arthur's room without being seen and to pour the water over his head. Taken by surprise, Arthur gave a start and Noara cried out for joy. His soul had re-entered his body and he was saved.

Arthur shrugged. Of course he felt better. But he credited the antibiotics the doctor had given him.

Noara keeps her faith in the deductive powers of the diviner and the power of his *tangande*. She will go back to consult him whenever anyone in the family falls ill.

Dear Noara! Throughout her youth she had seen everyone she knew run to the diviner when someone fell ill. She had just married Naba Kobré when a Mission was opened in the neighboring village and a dispensary set up. Gradually,

41

the mothers she knew began to bring their babies there, and she realized that fewer of them died than before (actually the mortality rate dropped fifty per cent). But now the hospital was in town, ten miles from the village. If a person was very ill when he was brought there, he died. Then what good was it? That was the way Noara reasoned.

But the young people are anxious for more dispensaries and hospitals. In some areas there is only one doctor for forty or fifty thousand inhabitants, and most African governments would welcome the help of the more developed countries in spreading their medical services.

Another of my friends belongs to a wealthy Yoruba family. Monica was born in Dahomey and attended the Sisters' school. She liked sewing best, and so did an apprenticeship in one of the better dressmaking establishments in Porto-Novo. She then married Peter John, a young cocoa planter, a Yoruba like herself, who lived in Nigeria. Mrs. John set up her own shop in Olorundo in Nigeria, where she now employs 20 apprentices. They pay a fee of ten shillings a month, or, if they are resident apprentices, two pounds sterling a month (about six dollars) for board and room. They learn all the fine points of dressmaking in three years. Some stay on two years longer to learn cutting and fitting. Since Mrs. John is very well known, a diploma from her establishment ensures a good clientele when the graduates return home.

The Johns have five children living. Three of their babies died in infancy. The oldest is studying in England, and a daughter attends the University of Ibadan. The third daughter, Mary, learned dressmaking from her mother. The two youngest children, both boys, are in secondary school.

42

I was invited to Mary's wedding, a lavish affair, for both families are well-to-do. The groom, Edward, is the son of a great Yoruba chief, with whom I had the privilege of sharing the "kola of friendship." After a very interesting conversation during a visit I had paid him, he signaled to a servant to bring the kolas, a tropical fruit. I broke open one of them and offered the pieces to the chief in my left hand. He took the piece nearest my wrist (that is the piece nearest the heart) and ate it. I then ate a piece and gave the rest to the three persons who were with us. By this gesture we cemented a sincere and lasting friendship.

But to get back to the wedding. For the church ceremony, Mary and Edward dressed in Western fashion, as did her parents and bridesmaids. But Edward's parents and his attendants were dressed in the handsome traditional costume. Both types of dress appeared among the other relatives and guests.

After the Mass and the congratulations outside the Church, everyone went to the bride's home for lunch. The big wedding dinner, however, was to take place in the evening. That afternoon we went to congratulate the bride at her home. She received us alone in her room. The groom was in town with his friends. The women of the house were busy with last minute preparations for the dinner and decorations for the long table in the courtyard. Mary showed us the classic "hope chest," which holds the trousseau every Yoruba must give his fiancée. It was a handsome chest of polished wood. In it lay her wedding dress and the dresses she would wear afterward. There were 30 in all . . . and she would wear a different one each Sunday to show everyone the love and the wealth of her bridegroom. The head kerchiefs to match each dress as well as her personal lingerie

43

were also gifts of the groom. She had bought herself hats, bags, perfumes, which were in a large chest with glass sides. The wedding gifts were displayed on two long tables — jewelry, silver, table linen, art objects. It was hard to believe we were in the Africa of the storybooks.

Mary was completely happy except for one family worry. Her Aunt Lucy and her daughter Frances who lived in Dahomey had not been able to come. This, too, was an old familiar story. Lucy was a widow. Her husband had died suddenly of a stroke four months before. His pagan relatives refused to believe it was a natural death. They accused Lucy of killing her husband, and — as custom permitted — took everything she had. She was then being subjected to all the cruelties of the ancient custom.

The doctor had diagnosed her husband's death as due to a cerebral hemorrhage, but he was a European and for those who keep the old ways a sudden death is not natural. According to customary law the widow is responsible. So, for the last four months Lucy had had to dress in a simple cloth of coarse weave and sleep on the bare floor of her room. Custom forbade her to go out or to comb her hair. At the time of the wedding this seclusion was to last another three months. If it had not been for her daughter Frances, she would have had no food.

I asked Mary if her Aunt's husband was a Yoruba.

No, he was an Adjibo, she said, but the same customs more or less were to be found in other tribes. In former times all widows of the deceased were made to take a poisoned drink to see which of them was responsible for the husband's death. It was the kind of trial by ordeal which was a common means of arriving at the "truth" in the Europe of the middle Ages. According to ancient popular tribal belief in Africa, the guilty one would die, or at least be very sick after drinking the poison, but the innocent would not suffer anything.

I asked Mary whether to her knowledge such trials by ordeal still took place.

Not officially, she told me, but one could not say that they had completely disappeared. In any case, the punishments imposed on the widows were still in force in certain regions and her aunt was a victim of them.

"But couldn't she refuse to obey the custom? Or couldn't she leave the place — take refuge here, for instance?"

"She was in such a state of shock at her husband's death that she did not even think to hide her money. And if she had run away, she would have given proof of her guilt and would have run the risk of being poisoned. . . . Mama is sending money to one of her friends, who gives it secretly to Frances. If my aunt's brothers-in-law knew about it they would beat Frances until she gave the money to them."

Mary's Aunt Lucy had two sons and another daughter, all studying in France. Frances was working for her baccalaureate at the Sisters' school in Cotonou and was on vacation when her father died. It was possible she might not be able to go back to school. Not only was she staying home to help her mother, but, since her father's family were insistent that customary law be followed, she now belonged to her father's brothers, who, according to Mary, were anxious to marry her off for a fat dowry.

According to tribal law, she had no right to refuse. And in the present circumstances, her uncles would not listen to her in any case. While the mourning period lasted, any resistance on her part would only make her mother's lot more painful. Besides, she was trying to gain time. . . .

45

Young girls have not yet achieved freedom everywhere.

We could well sympathize with Mary's concern. I did not know her aunt, but I knew many others who had suffered in similar fashion. There was Sérère, for example, who on returning from her husband's funeral watched his brothers carry off all she had. They even emptied the food cooking over the fire in order to take the pot with them, for it was a new one.

"Didn't you protest?" I had asked her.

"I did not say anything," she replied. "The pot belonged to them like all the other things."

I remembered Augustina, a Christian, who refused to marry her dead husband's brother, who was a pagan and already married. He was threatening to take her children from her if she did not give in.

Change seems slow in coming when those close to one are suffering. Only legislation will help to accelerate it.

As for Frances, I guessed that her uncles had already promised her in marriage, and perhaps had already received some installment of the bride price. It was some consolation to me, however, to think that she could find protection in the Mandel decree of June 15, 1939, and that the battle I had helped to fight before the war to obtain for African women the minimal liberty of being able to refuse a husband chosen for them by others or imposed on them by force would be of use to still another of them.

The drums for the dead had been beating all night. It must be a notable who has died, we thought. Perhaps it was Tingan Dabire, the chief of the village of Lissa. He had been sick for three weeks although we thought he had begun to improve.

In midmorning, a woman came to our medical center with the news. It was indeed Tingan. He had in fact been improving, but his first wife consulted a diviner who gave her a potion to cure him. Since Tingan had already taken the white doctor's medicine, the potion made him more ill again. He had died the evening before after being baptized by one of his sons, Peter, who was a secretary to the District Commissioner.

We learned afterward that the European doctor, whom Peter summoned, had recognized the symptoms of poisoning and requested permission to perform an autopsy. But the family refused. To bring a diviner to trial would expose the whole family to the risk of poisoning sooner or later.

That afternoon we went to offer our condolences to the family. The body of the dead chief was seated in state near his house on a platform overlooking the assemblage of mourners. A mat covered with cloths formed a canopy to protect the corpse from the hot rays of the sun. On the platform were piled all his clothes, Western style suits and African robes, his headdresses and the insignia of his chiefdom. Nearby was the funeral orchestra made up of six huge drums that beat the death knell and eight xylophones that accompanied the funeral chant. Each newcomer was led to the platform where he greeted the deceased with the cry, "Sa, we!" (Come, Father!) and then took his place in the crowd. The chant praising the virtues of the deceased rose and fell. The men began the funeral dance in his honor. Their turn finished, the women rose and danced their tribute to their dead chief. Suddenly there was the sound of a whistle and then complete silence. The Mission catechist began the recitation of the rosary and the Christians among the mourners gave the responses. Then the funeral dance

47

began again, and once more the chant of the mourners rose and fell, rose and fell.

When the rosary ended, we entered the chief's house. His brothers and several of his sons were seated together in silence. His widows and other relatives were in another room. All of them had a thin cord, made of bark for the men and of black fiber for the women, tied around one wrist. The Dagari believe that grief at the death of a loved one can induce a member of the family to commit suicide. Therefore a friend accompanies each member of the family everywhere, holding him by this leading string, as it were, to keep him from doing himself harm.

Tingan was survived by eleven widows. The four oldest had whitened their faces, arms and bodies with kaolin, for this is the distinctive mark of widows. The other seven had refused to perform the ceremonies that accompany the preparation of the kaolin, thereby signifying their desire to become Christian.

Tingan Dabire, a pagan and polygamous, had great sympathy for Catholicism. For the past ten years he had had all his children baptized and had permitted his older children to choose whether they wished to become Christian or not. Twenty-two of them had. With some surprise I recognized among the women wearing the mourning cord, Margareta, whose son is a teacher and whose two daughters are nurses at our Mission. After expressing my sympathy, I asked her if she was related to the deceased. He was her brother, she answered. Was she the daughter of the old chief, then?

Margareta smiled. No, he was her father's "brother" because their fathers were brothers. Her great-grandfathers had the same father. That was the way the relationship was handed down.

Since Margareta knew me well, I asked her what would become of Tingan's widows. According to tribal custom they would be inherited by Tingan's sons. But Peter had told his father that to become a Christian he must renounce polygamy and free his wives. So Tingan had declared, before everyone present, that his wives were free, and after that Peter had baptized him. That was why some of the widows had refused to cover themselves with kaolin. This was forbidden by the Mission because of the ceremonies that accompanied it. All the widows would stay in Tingan's house until the mourning period was over, and then they would be free to return to their father's home or to marry again, choosing someone either from among the members of the family or outside the family.

Those who had covered themselves with kaolin were the wives Tingan had inherited from his father.

"Since they are old," Margareta said, "they are afraid no one will take care of them. By putting on the kaolin they have shown that they wish to be inherited according to the tribal custom. In this way, they will be able to remain in their own house, and nothing in their lives will be changed."

The other widows would not find it too difficult to re-marry, she assured me. They were still young, ranging in age from 25 to 36. "There are still many men between 30 and 40 years of age who haven't been able to marry because of polygamy," Margareta observed.

"I know," I replied, "but I thought they did not care to marry widows."

"Oh, they'd prefer a young girl, certainly; but when they cannot afford one, they are glad enough to marry a young widow who has already borne children, and so they know they will have children too."

49

"But Tingan's children?"

"They belong to his family, according to our custom. That is why widows always remarried within their husband's family before the missionaries came."

"Can they actually choose their new husband among the heirs?"

"They do now, if they are Christian, but this is contrary to our old custom. Formerly, if a widow asked to be given to a specific heir she would be suspected of having already given herself to him during her husband's lifetime, and she would be severely punished."

Among the Dagari in former times it was the custom to ask the corpse who had caused its death, and then the guilty person was killed. But that is no longer done.

"It is not too good to be a widow!" I reflected.

"For child widows, it can sometimes be a good thing, Sister," Margareta corrected me. "It was for me. My brother Gyregmwin had given me in marriage to a notable of Jirapa. I was six years old when I went to live in his house, and I was brought up by his first wife. Five years later my husband died. He was 58 years old; I was eleven. I was a widow before I ever married. I was inherited by one of his sons, George, who used to attend the Mission. He asked if I would like to go with him. I said yes. I felt very happy, I remember, because he had asked me what I wanted to do. That is how I happened to go to school and become a Christian. George was very good to me, and from time to time he brought me a present. When I was 16 years old, he asked me if I would be his wife. I was astonished for I was his wife by inheritance, and now I loved him all the more for his tact. He had treated me as a free person. We were married at the Mission, and you know that I have

50

always been happy with him. . . . You see, for me it was a good thing to be a widow!"

Margareta's case was not unusual. But not all stories of child widows in the past had as happy endings.

The custom of child betrothal is gradually disappearing among the Dagari, largely owing to Christian influence. Polygamy is gradually disappearing, too. A Christian girl is not betrothed before she is 15 or 16 years old — instead of at 5 or 6, as in former times — and greater freedom of choice tends to be granted the women.

Tingan had sons living in Kumasi, Accra, and Tamale. When it became certain he was going to die, they had been notified by wire and were expected in the evening because there was a flight that day from Accra to Tamale. The funeral was to take place the next morning. In former times, a dead chief was kept in state for three or four days, but this was too long a time, especially in the hot season. Now, the funeral usually takes place two days after the death.

I thanked Margareta for telling me so much, and we took our leave after having greeted again the mourning women seated about the dead fires. Since the day before, no food had been prepared in the house, and none would be until the funeral was over. But outside, great jars of millet beer were set out for all who came, relatives and friends, and at the edge of the courtyard, three or four mammy traders were busy frying pancakes. . . .

As we walked slowly back to the Mission my thoughts went to Accra, a bright bustling city with modern buildings and a magnificent university catering to over a thousand students. Within a few years, other old customs that still persist in many regions would gradually retreat before the advance of education, social service, and legislation. Would

51

the part Christianity had played and was still playing in this advance be remembered?

My own Europe had known many similar customs, practiced for centuries by our ancestors. The resemblance between African customary law and the ancient laws of Europe is pertinent to a comprehension of the transition taking place in Africa. A comparison between the two puts into proper perspective the contrast between an impatient educated elite and the illiterate mass. It becomes easier to understand how centuries-old customs, once legitimate, block the path of a new youth desirous to make its own way, and also how the result is disorder and anarchy when all customs and traditions, even the best and most valid of them, are abandoned.

Between the two extremes, there is room for harmonious change, which will foster a true flowering of African civilization enriched by Christianity and other new influences.

As Leopold Senghor has so rightly said, "Every great civilization is a hybrid civilization." Western civilization itself is a classic example of this. Africa seeks only to make her own the universal values in other cultures; her people, of course, want technical progress, industrialization, the development of their resources. But above all they want the. intellectual, social and spiritual advancement of all levels of the population for they know, in the words of Senghor, "That a civilization founded only on technical and material progress is an anti-civilization," and permits no one — whether African, European, or American — completely to fulfill his human destiny.

3. The Traditional African Family

We know from history that before nations came into being, there existed across the world more or less powerful *families,* which were homogeneous societies and possessed all the prerogatives of a modern state. They lived by hunting, fishing, and gathering wild fruits, and after cultivating the land until it was exhausted, they migrated elsewhere in search of new and fertile lands until they finally settled permanently in a specific territory.

These families were not the father-mother-children nucleus we think of today, but included the whole family group, gathering in all the descendants of the same ancestor and strongly bound together under the authority of the head, or chief, of the family.

In the Western world this type of family now belongs to the past and the individual household (father, mother, children) constitutes an independent family unit both socially and before the law. In sub-Saharan Africa, the individual household — monogamous or polygamous — also exists. But it is attached to the family group by extremely strong

53

legal, social, and economic bonds. More than half the population of sub-Saharan Africa still belongs to this type of family organization, which after all is still in existence in the Near East and was at one time typical of ancient Europe, both throughout the Roman empire and in the Anglo-Saxon countries. In England it persisted until the thirteenth and fourteenth centuries and in some areas of Scotland until the eighteenth.

In the traditional African family the father or grandfather, uncle or great uncle is the head and center. He has authority over his wives, children and grandchildren, and over their wives and children. His word is law for all of them, especially while they live within the same compound. It is he who makes the important decisions affecting his younger brothers, their wives, their married sons and their wives and children. His authority is that of master, priest, judge, and father. It is a domestic monarchy, not unlike that governed in ancient Rome by the *patria potestas*.

The determination of kinship also recalls the customs of ancient Rome, for the family institution in both hinges on direct lineal descent. In other words, the family includes all the descendants of the same ancestor, but only through the father's *or* the mother's lineage according to whether it is a patriarchal or matriarchal society. The former recognizes only patrilineal descent (the *agnatio* of the Romans) while the latter consider their kinsmen all those descended from the same ancestor on the mother's side. Among these the maternal lineage is the only family bond and alone has legal consequences.

But while the old Roman family was monogamous, the traditional African family permits more than one wife. Polygamy thus increases the number of collateral kinsmen among whom the bonds of blood relationship are reinforced by the juridical ties binding the family group. The same title of respect — "father" or "grandfather" — may thus be given various members of one generation, the same courtesy and submission shown them all, and their wives addressed as "grandmother" or "mother." An African will also give the title mother (sometimes aunt) to all the wives of his real father, and sometimes also to the sisters of his own mother. A whole series of questions is often necessary in order to learn the true father and mother of an African.

I once asked one of my West African friends, Perpetua by name, who the woman was so busily grinding millet beside her.

"She is my mother," she answered. Since the woman seemed almost as young as Perpetua herself, I persisted: "Is she your own mother?"

Then she laughed. "She is my love-mother. That is what we call the woman we have chosen as mother when our own mother has died, or lives too far away. We also call a woman who has brought us up our mother, even if she is not a relative."

It is equally difficult to learn the degree of kinship between persons of the same generation, for the same word denotes older brothers and cousins, while still another word is used for younger brothers and cousins. What is important in Africa is not the degree of kinship but of seniority. Is he an older relative to whom I owe respect and who has the right to command me, or is this a younger relative who will respect and obey me?

One day among the Mossi I was talking to Louis, the son of a great chief, when a young woman came to him with a request. After she had gone I inquired who she was.

"She is my sister, Tanfisi," he answered.

"Is she one of the daughters of the chief, then?"

"No, she is his sister, too."

At my blank look, Louis gave me a fine paternal smile and launched into an explanation. His grandfather had in his old age married a young girl of fifteen named Nobila, who had borne him a daughter, Tanfisi. He died shortly afterward and his eldest son, Lalle, who succeeded to the chiefdom, took Nobila as his wife. They had a son who attended the Mission and was baptized Louis. This was my young tutor. Lalle and Tanfisi had the same father; Louis and Tanfisi had the same mother. Therefore, she was the sister of both of them.

Everywhere in Africa, the bonds of kinship remain strong as long as the memory of the common ancestor is preserved. It is common to find whole villages, or large sections of a village, in which all the inhabitants are related and are therefore subject to the same head of the family. In addition, all those who have the same totem or who offer sacrifice to the same Ancestor consider themselves kin one to another, with all the rights and duties this implies.

While there is no legal bond linking the members of a patriarchal family to their mother's family and vice versa, blood relationship is an impediment to marriage with the nearest of kin; but this is true only in certain tribes and only for those kindred specified by the local law.

In matriarchal families the father has only limited authority over his own children; legally they belong to their mother's family. The head of that family, however, is always a man — the maternal uncle or grand uncle who has charge over the children of all women in the family. In practice, decisions regarding the children are usually the responsibility of their maternal uncle, and succession is also matrilineal. In such families children have no right to inherit their father's property. At his death it falls to a brother, if he was born of the same mother, or else to his sister's children.

In the Ivory Coast one day, two young boys were brought to the Mission school by their father. The next day their maternal uncle came to fetch them in a great state of irritation.

"These children belong to me," he said to the startled Sisters, "and I will not allow them to be sent to school without my advice." The following week the same gentleman returned and asked that his nephews be enrolled in the school. The Sister in charge ventured to ask him why he had taken the boys out of school the week before if he intended to bring them back.

"These boys are my sister's children," he gravely explained, "and therefore I am responsible for their education. I had to remind their father of that; this is not his affair. He must take care of his sister's children."

There are other West African tribes that more or less combine both orders of kinship. The paternal lineage is passed on only through the male members of the family, and the maternal only through the women. The children of two brothers, therefore, are "related" and so are the children of two sisters; but cross cousins — i.e., the children of a brother and those of his sister — have no bond of kinship between them.

With each generation, the children and grandchildren widen the family circle, but never break it to start a new family. It is the Roman *gens,* the African clan, composed of those born free. The head of the family can, as in ancient

Rome, attach clients to the family. These may be freed slaves or strangers who ask his protection. They then become legally associated with the clan according to a bond similar to that of the *gens* in ancient Rome.

A sovereign juridical entity, the clan has its own life and its own boundaries; it forms a whole, which before the Europeans came was self-sufficient in a closed economy. What it wanted from its neighbors it took by war or obtained through interclan agreements.

In certain regions the association of several clans, or the continued development of a large and prosperous clan through the subjection of its neighbors, formed kingdoms whose social structure kept the same basic features as the family clan.

This was also true in Rome in the period preceding the Republic. The king was chief of the army, judge in the city, priest in charge of the State religion, just as the *paterfamilias* was head of the clan, judge in his home or *domus,* priest in charge of family worship. The same organization existed among the Germanic tribes and in the early Anglo-Saxon kingdoms. There are many points of resemblance between them and the kingdoms still in existence in sub-Saharan Africa.

Like the successive waves of invasion through the old Roman Empire, the various migrations, which through the centuries modified the political power of the different clans, seem to have left their internal structure unchanged. Today they have lost the sovereignty they once enjoyed, but they still keep the memory of old alliances and conflicts, and the latter give rise at times to a renewal of hostility and even murderous fighting which one might think had been ended forever.

Socially and politically, the clan is opening to outside influences. But its inner law is changing much more slowly and is still practically unchanged in regions where foreign influence has been slight.

In its earliest stages, the clan (comprising at the most 200 or 300 persons) was gathered into one vast compound like a fort, with one the gate barricaded at night by heavy logs. Enclosures like this are still to be found in northern regions of the Ivory Coast, Ghana, Togo, and Dahomey, but today many of them gather in 30 to 50 persons or less. The young generation prefers more freedom and privacy in separate houses.

On the other hand, the clan may extend through one or more villages, surrounded in former times by a wall of enclosure with one gate, like the *tatas* of the Mali, which can still be found here and there in certain areas.

The head of the clan is the "legal father" of all its members, descendants like himself of a common ancestor. In addition he is the intermediary and the link between the clan and the assembly of ancestors; for the latter continue to live in the next world and to watch over their descendants, inspiring and guiding the decisions of the chief.

He does not govern alone, however, the most important decisions being taken in accord with the family elders. In the past these included decisions to make war on another clan or a neighboring village (provided the clan was not part of a federated kingdom) to punish crimes (robbery, murder) either by flogging, binding in chains, mutilation, or even death in the most serious cases. These rights are no longer recognized by the governmental authorities but it would be hazardous to say they no longer exist. Cases are not unknown in which families have punished with death

59

one or another member because of an offense against the customary law.

For in old African customary law, as in that of the ancient Germanic tribes, the clan bears the collective responsibility for the conduct of each of its members. A clan offended by a great theft committed against it (a theft of livestock, for instance) or the murder of one of its members, does not itself undertake to punish the culprit but lays its claim for adequate compensation before the culprit's clan. It is up to the latter to judge him and to punish him as it sees fit.

Even today, Africans prefer to bring all matters concerning the family before the family court — for example, the punishment of an adulterer or of a young man whose repeated thefts have brought dishonor on the family, sending away a woman accused of thieving or witchcraft, cursing a serious offender out of the family.

The curse of a chief is a feared and fearsome punishment. It deprives its object of all contact with his people. He no longer has any right to help from them and he cannot remain in any village inhabited by members of the family. He must go alone among strangers, where he may or may not meet a cordial welcome. In former times he often became a slave. Now the towns afford a place of refuge, but he will not be received or helped by members of his clan who may be living there, nor by those of other clans which are friendly to his.

It is easy to understand why an African feared this curse more than death. To escape it he preferred to obey even the orders of which he disapproved. But this curse is becoming increasingly rare. The African who does not agree with his chief moves to a town and this dispenses him from obeying without having to declare a direct refusal. "The donkey that kicks against a stone," the Africans say, "only ruins his hoofs."

Obedience as well as respect for the chief is quite general. Custom prescribes that his authority must protect the common good, and in those regions where the traditional custom still prevails, the power of a good chief is protective and benevolent. With the disruption of old patterns some chiefs have become excessively authoritarian, with a lack of regard for the aspirations of the younger generation. But when this happens it is actually an abuse of the custom, the young people feel frustrated and take off in large numbers for the urban centers, ostensibly to earn money for taxes and for the bridal dowry but in reality to achieve a little more personal liberty and to escape the restraints imposed by the custom.

In a large clan that is subdivided into several family groups, the chief still has authority over major decisions but leaves to the chief of each subgroup or compound the responsibility for his wives, brothers, sons and their wives, children and servants, together with the duty of assigning the daily chores and similar preoccupations.

In rural areas each woman of the group ordinarily cultivates the amount of land necessary to feed herself and her children. In the savanna, where cultivation is not possible except during the short rainy season, a man with two or more wives divides the work of cultivation between them. He keeps the harvest and later doles out each morning enough millet for the day's meals.

After contributing the work share prescribed by custom, every member of the family — man, woman, and adolescent — may cultivate a plot of land for himself or engage in trade or other occupation, such as weaving, pottery making, basket making and trading, making soap, etc. The proceeds belong to him except for certain prescribed gifts. For example, in Northern Ghana and the Upper Volta, a woman who makes millet beer must give a jug of it to her husband. If he wants more than that he must pay for it like any other purchaser. But if the millet used in making the beer belongs to him he has a right to all the proceeds from its sale and the wife can claim nothing as salary for her work.

Where cotton is cultivated each woman has her own personal field. She spins the cotton during the dry season and according to custom must give her husband a new garment every year. She gives the weaver enough spun cotton for two garments: he returns one to her and keeps the other as wages for his work.

The compound chief is subject to the clan chief for everything that involves the future of the family, such as the marriage of a child, taking on any indebtedness or making a sizable loan. He cannot sell any cultivable land, for this belongs to the whole family. The clan chief cannot sell it either unless all the family elders agree.

At the death of a clan chief, the entire succession falls to one of his brothers (that is to say the nearest collateral relative) or his eldest son, depending on the tribe, and the latter then becomes the "juridical father" of all the members of the clan. In matriarchal families, the heir is a brother of the deceased (if they were born of the same mother) or the eldest son of his sister.

The heir may marry the widows of the deceased, but ordinarily he takes only one or two of them and assigns the others among the dead chief's other brothers and sons. In certain tribes, however, a son may not marry his father's widows. In others, a man cannot marry the widows of a younger brother. On the other hand, younger sons always have the right, and sometimes the duty, to marry the widows of their older brothers or cousins. This is to their advantage, especially when the widow is young, for then they acquire a wife without having to pay the bridal dowry or fulfill other obligations.

It is not hard to understand what a severe test this custom can be for a Christian who is already married when he inherits the wife of his older brother — or even several wives if the brother was not Christian. To marry them is a distinct material advantage, especially if he has a large farm or coffee plantation, for then he will acquire that many more workers he does not have to pay. If he does not marry his brother's widow, another heir will. And if his brother has given a high bride price for her, he may reason: "Should I just throw all that money away?" Only the deeply convinced Christians refuse to become polygamists in such cases.

The widows and the young children of the deceased generally have no right to any of the property he has left, but they are not abandoned. They remain within the family circle and the mother's new husband must treat the children of the deceased as his own.

This family solidarity is very strong in areas where the ancestral custom still prevails. If some member of the family earns more than the others, then he must make sure all the members benefit from it. If he is condemned to pay a big fine the whole clan will help him, and so on. On the other hand he must help the other members of his clan when they are in need. This explains the great sense of attachment that the African has to his clan and his dependence upon it. In it he finds security, help and affection, but with no sense of inferiority; he is the equal of the other members of his generation, who depend, like him, on the elders.

More than half the population of sub-Saharan Africa are farmers. In the savanna, the size of the crops depends on the rainfall.

Inhabitants of a given region ordinarily have the same level of living, which varies from poverty to relative comfort with no great wealth or marked class distinctions. The rest of the population are shepherds and artisans (smiths, cordwainers, shoemakers, minstrels, etc.). In certain areas, like the Mali Republic, these sometimes comprise a closed caste, often despised although richer than the farmers.

In still other areas, there is an aristocracy of chiefs and warriors, once powerful and still with considerable prestige and influence. I once asked a chief's son what distinguished the nobles from the rest of the people in his particular tribe. "The nobles," he answered, "are those who know the history and genealogy of their families. The rest know only their grandparents."

In the family so constituted, the chief alone has a complete juridical personality. It is he who decides on the principal activities of the family in general and of the individual in particular. Whether it is a question of attending school, choosing a career, enlisting in the army, or getting married, the clan chief, using his sovereign right, designates this or that member of the family, whether they are his own children, those of his brothers, or the descendants of former slaves. Strictly speaking (and this was the same in ancient Europe) he does not even have to consult the father of the interested party, still less the individual himself, although new concepts are influencing him more and more to do so.

This family organization, which in Europe and elsewhere

was the earliest form of social organization, still exists in the interior of tropical Africa, and it governs the lives of the greater part of the population. Details of form may differ from one region to another, according to the internal development of the juridical institutions, the climate, the natural resources of the country, its economic organization, the availability of transportation, the indigenous religion, the influence of neighboring clans and the degree of Islamic or Christian penetration. But on the whole the family structure changes more slowly than the social and political institutions.

The coastal areas, however, present a different picture. Here there has been contact with Europe since the sixteenth century, when the Portuguese established ports of call in the Gulf of Guinea. Then came the Dutch, the British, the Germans, the French, to install their posts in the same regions. Trade in gold, ivory, gum, and, unhappily, in slaves too, assured their fortune.

They took wives in the country. Some prolonged their stay and like the wealthier local chiefs took several wives. Some afterward left these wives behind when they returned to their own countries, but many remained and they bequeathed to the especially intelligent populations of these areas a ferment of family evolution which, developing through new contacts with Western ways, gave rise to that middle class along the coast whose superiority and shrewd business sense impress everyone who visits them.

In the nineteenth century, the suppression of slavery freed a great number of Africans who had adopted the religion and customs of their European or American masters. Philanthropic societies assumed the task of taking them back to Africa. Freetown, the capital of Sierra Leone, was founded in 1787 by slaves freed in the British territories. In 1822 freed slaves from the United States were transported to the coast of West Africa, where they soon dominated the native population and gradually built Monrovia, the capital of Liberia. After the suppression of slavery in South America, other freedmen regained a homeland in Africa, settling mostly in Dahomey and Nigeria. These "Brazilians" as they are still called there, have often kept as their family name the name of their former masters or that of the city in which they lived. Both introduced new customs into Africa, especially crafts and more modern methods, which helped to improve practically every aspect of the living standard — housing, clothing, industries, furniture, hand crafts, and so forth. These new populations, like the Europeans who had founded families in Africa, were used to the Latin concept of paternal authority. In addition, they either had no ties with the local clans or attached little importance to them. The father therefore exercised over his own children, and sometimes over unmarried next of kin, the rights and duties of his authority. But all considered that marriage emancipated the new spouse in some way and withdrew his children from the direct authority of their grandfather, although respect for him required that his advice be taken into account in all that concerned the family.

The example of these families had a modifying influence on the family law of the whole coastal area, although the level of living still differed according to class, wealth, education.

In the cities of southern Ghana, southern Togo and southern Dahomey, as in the old sections of Lagos and in the Yoruba towns of Nigeria, one finds houses of mudbrick and baked brick side by side. The mudbrick homes are covered with a layer of cement which improves appearance and increases stability. Their furnishings parallel those of an American middle class family, and the mistress of the house, if you win her confidence, will tell you something of the family history. She may perhaps tell you about a grandfather (Dutch, Swiss, or British) whose picture hangs in the room, or about her grandmother of Portuguese descent; about a sister living in Sierra Leone, a brother in London, another in America, a daughter married and living in Senegal, another studying in Paris. . . .

Close by this cement-covered house, one of plain mud brick takes us back into old ways of life. Within it, straw mats serve for beds and chairs. Gay cloths hang from a rope stretched across the room and, even if the men of the house can speak French or English, the women generally speak only the local dialect. These people are very close to the populations of the interior, for they live apart from the aristocratic bourgeoisie whose "old families" carefully keep their own traditions and privileges.

Since the beginning of the twentieth century another bourgeoisie has come into being and increases each year. This is made up of the new educated elite. Its members come from all sections of the population. They may be sons of farmers or of chiefs, born in bush villages or in the comfortable town house of a wealthy family, but they have attended secondary or technical schools or the university. Their intelligence and perseverence have enabled them to achieve an honorable position. Government officials, ministers, doctors, teachers, technicians, employees in business, customary chiefs, they are natural leaders to whom the people listen and who excercise a great influence.

But whatever their position they are still under the authority of the head of the family if they are young and belong to a homogeneous clan. The latter imposes new duties on them: they must help all their kin rise up the social ladder and pursue the studies necessary to obtain similar positions. This family solidarity can be a heavy burden when only one member has achieved a better position than his relatives. He must take their children into his home if they are sent to him in order to continue their studies or to find work in the city. Even a handsome salary is not enough to provide for them all adequately, and as a result the youngsters may sometimes suffer from malnutrition. But even when it is a burden, the African cordially takes in all his clan members who come to him and helps them as much as he can, even at the cost of personal sacrifice and inconvenience.

Today, however, the young people normally aspire to more individual freedom than their elders enjoyed. They have a concept of family life and of conjugal unity unknown to preceding generations. They have ordinarily solved these family problems for themselves by adopting certain Western customs. They understand that the masses have the same desires, and they hope for a modification of the customary marriage which will take into account modern ideas while preserving the values which have given the African family its strength and stability.

4. Betrothal and Marriage in Customary Law

In modern Western societies, marriage marks the start of a new family, with its own autonomy and patrimony. In African societies, where the family in the strict sense is but a part of the global (extended) family of the clan, marriage does not create a new social organism. It is the means necessary to ensure posterity. In traditional Africa, as in ancient Europe, the young woman given in marriage takes her place in a family already constituted in order to contribute to its increase.

She is sometimes the second, third, fourth, or even the fifth wife, but even if she is the first, she does not form a new family with her husband. She is still a member of her own family of origin.

This concept of marriage was common to all ancient civilizations. It prevailed in ancient Rome and among the Anglo-Saxon peoples of medieval times. There are in fact numerous resemblances among these diverse legislations, which seem so far removed in time and space, suggesting, at it were, a common origin of all peoples, who maintained

69

similar institutions despite their being scattered throughout the world. Through the centuries, juridical modifications have been made in African customary law as in Western legislation, accentuating the differences.

Among certain African populations influenced by Islam, there has been an admixture of Koranic law with customary law. More recently, Africa's entrance into world economy has upset its social and family structures, which had their origin in a different economic system. And finally, the influence of the Western way of life, particularly on Africans who have lived in Europe or America, as well as conversion to Christianity, have contributed to a change in concepts of marriage and married life.

But before considering these transformations, it will be useful to review briefly African marriage law as a whole, for it still regulates more than half the people of sub-Saharan Africa.

In Africa as in all ancient civilizations, marriage is an important social and juridical event, an alliance between two families of primary interest to the heads of those families. Its purpose is to increase, through numerous offspring, the prosperity of the clan, its numerical strength, the fullness of its life. The choice of the woman or women to fulfill this role rests primarily with the head of the family.

The clan chief, whose duty it is to ensure the well-being and the permanence of his group, has also the duty, therefore, of securing suitable brides for the young men of the clan. He makes his request to friendly families of honorable reputation who have distinguished themselves in the local history. At the same time, when he promises young girls of his clan in marriage, he does so only after informing himself about the families in which they will live, learning if the women are well treated and the family circumstances are comfortable.

It is the clan chief who after carefully weighing all the factors decides upon the marriages, knowing full well that the parties concerned will ratify his decision by a simple acceptance of it. A common saying of the Marka tribe of Mali underlines a bit wryly the power of the family chiefs: "The father always chooses the first wife of his son, even if she is one-eyed, and he always chooses his daughter's first husband, even if he is a leper."

For a young man it is an advantage to secure a wife without having to fulfill by himself all the customary obligations. For a girl it is an honor and a guarantee that she is entering a friendly clan that enjoys popular esteem. In any event, the communal family organization, together with polygamy, separates men and women in the daily round; and the young bride will have more frequent contacts with the women in her new home than with her husband. These marriages, so similar to those of an older Europe, seem to have been successful enough in former times.

Precise laws and customs — which vary somewhat from village to village and family to family — govern African marriage. Everywhere, kinship through direct descent is an impediment to marriage. Tribal laws vary regarding marriage with the next of kin by collateral descent. In some regions, difference of caste is likewise an impediment. It is necessary to have attained the age of puberty for marriage but not for betrothal. Finally, the consent of the parents, or the clan chiefs or whoever according to custom exercises authority over the future couple is considered more important than that of the spouses. Their consent in fact is not always a requirement for the validity of the marriage.

71

We might recall that in ancient Rome, the *paterfamilias* had the right to marry children off even against their will. Up to the second century he could, if he wished, dissolve the marriage of a son or daughter. It was not until the reign of Marcus Aurelius (at the end of the second century) that the consent of the spouses was required.

In his *English Social History*, G. M. Trevelyan writes: "In the Middle Ages, the choice of partners for marriage had normally nothing whatever to do with love; the Pastons and other county families regarded the marriages of their children as counters in the game of family aggrandizement, useful to buy money and estates, or to secure the support of powerful patrons. . . ." In France and other European countries until 50 or 100 years ago, marriages were arranged by the parents, especially among the wealthier classes. It is not at all strange that similar customs still prevail through much of the African continent. There are tribes in which the absolute power of the family head is still exercised as in ancient times and his choice imposed on both the young men and the young women. But there are others, more numerous, in which the spouses ratify the arrangements made for them either by express consent or more often by tacit acceptance when the girl is brought to her husband's home.

The marriage is generally preceded by a long period of betrothal. For a first marriage, the betrothal contract is concluded by the chiefs of the two young people. For a second marriage, the arrangements are made, with some exceptions, by the future groom. In some areas of the West African interior a man may engage in negotiations with one of his friends for a young girl, already born or about to be born, in order to cement the friendship existing between them.

"My friend, I am very fond of you; when your wife bears a little girl, she shall be for me," he says. When the child arrives, her father goes to his friend and says, "Your wife is born." Then, the friend in great content brings a gift to the child's mother. When the little one is five or six years old, he takes her into his home and entrusts her to his mother, or to his first wife, who will bring her up for him. A bride for a son is often requested in the same way.

Along the coast, in Ghana, Togo, Dahomey, women who are traders and earn money of their own often undertake the negotiations for a bride for a son or grandson. One of my friends in Dahomey told me how his grandmother had arranged his betrothal, having asked for the hand of a baby girl a few weeks old. Two bottles of liquor, a sum equivalent to ten dollars, a packet of matches and one of tobacco had sealed the contract. A few months later, this provident grandmother announced the good news to her grandson. He was thirteen years old, and he happily began to pay his court with small gifts for his future mother-in-law and his six-month-old fiancée. When she was about nine years old, she was told: "Here is your husband." And she was very happy because she already loved him.

The gifts of the future husband became larger each year, until finally he produced the presents expected at that time of every young man in his circumstances: twenty-four bottles of whiskey, two young goats, and the "hope chest" with twenty-four cloths for his bride, a number of kerchiefs, perfume, brilliantine, and various accessories. The bride price — the equivalent of $100 (some of it borrowed) — was given the girl's father. There was then a great feast at the groom's expense and three months later the "marriage feast" again brought the two families together.

73

In certain tribes (i.e., the Mande of Guinea and Mali) an intermediary is required who assumes all the customary negotiations, serves as a link between the two families, and if necessary as a witness in case of eventual litigation.

Most often the first step — whether it is taken by the family chief, the future groom, or the intermediary — is accomplished in a symbolic act. The suitor brings to the girl's guardian a bundle of wood, a rooster to be sacrificed on the occasion of a pagan feast, kola nuts, a beverage (millet beer, palm wine, or a number of bottles of liquor). Sometimes he also brings a cloth, a new hat, or some similar article. In Northern Ghana, the intermediary among the Dagari asks for this or that young girl to "carry the little brother of X . . ." (the future husband). A Gurunsi suitor says: "I have no one to draw water for me, and so I have come to you. . . ." Each tribe has its own formula and special customs which must be strictly observed. If the girl is already promised to someone else, or if the suitor is not acceptable, he is told: "Take your gift; I cannot accept it."

If the suit is taken into consideration, there is no answer. The men in the girl's family must be consulted and first of all the clan chief, if the suit was not addressed to him personally. The matter must be given some reflection and inquiries made about the young man's antecedents and those of his family. In certain tribes, there is then a religious ceremony: the father, or the family chief consults the ancestors or the guardian spirits of the family to see whether or not they consent to the alliance. Sometimes the young man's father also consults the ancestors before taking the first step.

At the suitor's second visit, the answer is again given in symbolic fashion. "You have treated me well; I shall treat you well" is the Mossi formula. In certain Mande tribes the answer is: "The rats have eaten the kolas." This means that the kolas and the beverages have been consumed by all the members of the family, who have thus been apprised of the marriage proposal. If later the betrothal is broken off or there is a divorce, the preliminary gifts are never restored, whatever their value was.

The betrothal period varies from two to fifteen years, according to the age of the girl when the contract was made. During this time the fiancé or members of his family must pay visits to his future in-laws at regular intervals set by custom, bringing with them the prescribed gifts. The groom in addition offers gifts to his fiancé appropriate to her age and lends her family such services as may be expected of a good son-in-law. Often the girl goes to spend periods of time with her mother-in-law, when she is not sent to live with her permanently. The future couple can thus grow to know each other and even to fall in love, especially when the age difference is not too great and the young man is thoughtful in the services he renders to the girl and her mother. If there is too great incompatibility between them, it is possible to break off the engagement, also according to customary law, but such instances seem to have been very rare in former times.

In the case of child betrothal, the girl is sometimes pledged to a specific young man, but in certain tribes the designation of her future husband is left undetermined until she reaches the age of puberty. Until then, the agreement is that a girl of one family is to marry a man of another family. The little girl is brought up in the family compound of her future husband which, it will be recalled, may number sixty to a hundred persons. She plays with the boys her own age, there are contacts with the older ones, and over the years the parents observe closely to which of their young men she is best suited. In these circumstances, too, a marriage of love is not unlikely. When the girl is fourteen years old, she is told, "This one will be your husband." She then returns to her own family to tell them the good news before undergoing the customary initiation rites. These last from six to twelve months, and at their completion she again returns to her own family, from where she is brought to the marriage feasts.

Whether the custom specifies the couple or the future husband himself has begun the marriage negotiations, if one of the betrothed happens to die before the time of the actual wedding, this does not dissolve the betrothal bond. The deceased is simply replaced by another member of his or her family, according to the custom. If there is no other member available at the moment, they say: "The mother is still there . . ." that is, a replacement may soon be born.

The marriage takes place only when the groom has fulfilled all the prescriptions of the tribal law. For a valid marriage, in fact, the girl's family must receive in exchange either another young girl or the bride price, or numerous and repeated services, unless, as in certain tribes, the validity of the marriage is regulated by some specific custom.

Marriage through the exchange of girls was probably the most ancient type in sub-Saharan Africa. Formerly, it obtained in a number of West African tribes. It was the usual form of marriage in the Southern Cameroun until the end of the past century.

In this type of marriage, two clans exchanged young women or girls. The future bridegroom could be designated when the contract was concluded or might remain unnamed until just before the marriage. The two weddings were rarely simultaneous, but after the first had taken place the other woman had to be given in exchange.

If this obligation was not carried out when the creditor family made its claim, then the first marriage was dissolved. If one of the two families recalled the bride, or if she left her husband, the other wife also had to leave her married home. The two divorces were correlative and almost simultaneous, even if the second couple involved had no reason to separate and even preferred to stay married.

Consequently, in West Africa the courts now try to dissociate the two marriages. They award, as an indemnity to the husband or the injured fiancé, a sum equivalent to the local bridal dowry of those who do not practice the exchange system. Some accept this indemnity and take a wife in a tribe with the bridal dowry system, or in a family that has replaced the exchange with the bride price. But if the fiancé or the injured husband or his parents do not accept this indemnity, their daughter or sister will refuse to return to her husband.

The Africans found other disadvantages in the exchange system and most tribes have given it up. The Bassa of the Southern Cameroun, for example, tell the following incident to explain how they came to change the customary practice.

Once upon a time, they say, the Elders made marriage consist in a simple exchange of girls. But this led only to trouble. For instance, there was a certain Banyak Boond, a notable of Nyeki, who took for his wife Ngondjek. In exchange he gave his sister Ngobanyak to Ndjek. This seemed to be an even exchange, but later it turned out to be nothing of the kind. In fact, Ngobanyak had six children, while Ngondjek had only two. Banyak's family called upon Ndjek to give up two of his children, so that then each family would have four. If not, Ngobanyak would return to her own family with all six, and Ngondjek would be sent home with her two.

The same story was repeated at Nyanga and in other villages. The Elders, concerned for the well-being of the country, were deeply moved and having gathered together in a kind of plenary assembly, they proclaimed: "*Mulga Masaki*, down with the exchange of young girls; let us put an end to these ancient customs, for they are leading the country to ruin by undermining the stability of marriage." The remedy was quick in coming. With the bartering of brides ended, the bride price began, that is to say, the giving of gifts in exchange. These consisted of a goat or two, slaves, if there were any, a native gun, gunpowder, salt. These last were items within everyone's means.

This does not mean, however, that in all instances the bride price system came about as a replacement for the barter system. On the contrary certain tribes have practiced the dowry custom for centuries. In some cases it may have supplanted the kidnaping of brides, which seems to have been one of the primitive forms of marriage in Africa as well as ancient Europe. The historical-legendary rape of the Sabine women by the subjects of Romulus is a case in point. But kidnaping always carried the risk of war, and as populations formed permanent settlements it was simpler to ask for a young girl, offering a compensation in exchange, i.e., either another girl or certain more or less valuable gifts.

Here again ancient European history offers examples of similar customs. The compensation consisted of a sum of money — a dowry — fixed by agreement between the parents of the couple, with or without the concurrence of other members of the family. With time, a uniform dowry was established and legally recognized throughout the particular region. The history of Germanic tribes and medieval English families contains abundant proof of this.

In African custom the dowry represents a `compensation and an homage to the power of the family chief, who thus cedes to the groom a share of his authority over the young girl and consequently of his paternal control over the children that will be born of her.

"From the time of the contract, the bride price is owed; the woman is owed," say the Manoe, of the Mali Republic.

The bride price is ordinarily paid by the father or the family of the groom in the first marriage; by the husband if he takes other wives afterward. I have, however, known a few young Africans who have been offered several wives by their father, mother, uncles, or aunts, all wealthy enough to pay the dowry for the son or nephew they wished to favor in a special way.

The African bride price, however, is not limited to money. There are numerous elements in it: loans, help with the farming, good offices of various kinds, not unlike the help and services rendered the bride's family in rural areas of Europe today which hardly attract notice. Then there are the customary gifts to the young girl and her parents, similar to those given in marriages without dowry but of a more obligatory nature, especially as to their value. These gifts are returned if the engagement is broken (unless the girl is recalled without reason by her parents or they refuse to give her up to her husband). Finally there is the bride price properly so-called, specified in former times by the custom: horned animals, foodstuffs, tools, money, and so forth.

In some regions, for example among the Dagari of Northern Ghana, the Lobi and Boussanse of Upper Volta, only cattle were used for the bride price a few years ago, as well as in sacrifices to the ancestors. They were neither sold at the market nor killed for food. A man with many daughters saw his herd grow with dowries received, and the capital thus acquired permitted him to obtain brides for his sons.

For example, Begyere, a Dagari, had six daughters. Since the dowry[1] for each was three cows, he eventually received eighteen cows, enabling him to pay the dowry for a bride for each of his four sons. Peter, on the other hand, had six sons and only two daughters. He needed eighteen cows to marry off his sons, while his daughters brought him only six. He was wealthy and had many cows anyway, so it did not matter. If he had been poor, he would have had to ask his brothers to lend him cows to meet the bride price requirement for his sons.

Before the turn of the century, when the dowry was still fixed and standardized by custom, it was uniform in almost every tribe and as a result was known to everyone. Besides, the marriages took place between families that were already allied in some way. It was common for a father to ask the same dowry for his daughter that he had given for her mother, and the closed economy in which these agricultural peoples lived protected them from any unjustified demands.

If as a consequence of personal or family reverses or a public calamity, a serious suitor could not pay all the dowry, he was given credit. This became for him a debt of honor which he paid as soon as possible unless more misfortune

---

[1] I have used "dowry" interchangeably with "bride price" in order to avoid repetition. In this context it is to be understood in the African sense — i.e., the gifts given by the groom to the bride's parents — and not the "dowry" the bride brings her husband in Western societies [*Trans. Note*].

overtook him. In that case, the debt passed to his children, who eventually completed the payment of their mother's bride price.

At the present time, the bride price has greatly increased in some West African areas. It is set in each case by the family chief or the girl's father, who, in contrast to former times, often requests enormous sums. This, as we shall see, may have serious social consequences. Young men cannot afford to marry on these terms, while older men who are wealthy and already polygamous can still acquire young brides. The latter would much prefer husbands their own age but are obliged by their families to go to the suitor who offers the most money.

The payment of the bride price and its acceptance confirm the accord between the two family heads; they do not signify the consent of the spouses. Where this consent is required, it is given in a symbolic fashion when the bride is led to her husband's home or in a ceremony shortly before the wedding, not when the bride price is paid, for this often is done in several installments. It sometimes happens that a part of the dowry is paid after the marriage, or even after the birth of several children. In most patriarchal tribes, the children can be claimed by the mother's family if the dowry has not been fully paid. In matriarchies — like the Serere of Senegal — each child of the marriage is taken by the mother's brother as soon as it is weaned and is not returned until the bride price payment is completed.

In case of divorce, the bride price must be refunded. "As long as the wife is alive, the husband has the right either to her or to the dowry," the Africans say. In a matriarchal tribe, the husband who requests or simply accepts the refund in divorcing his wife thereby loses all rights over his

81

children. These rights are limited, in any case, since the maternal uncle exercises the authority of head of the family.

There is a compensatory element in the bride price which is evident in many ways. In several West African tribes if the betrothal takes place when the girl is already grown the dowry will be larger, for then the fiancé will have helped his parents-in-law with the farming for a shorter time. It will be still higher if the fiancé is a city dweller and has given no help of this kind at all. If a Camerounian girl is brought up in her future husband's family, the dowry will be smaller than if she had remained with her own parents until her marriage.

The bride price is also a reciprocal affair. The parents who have received a number of presents from their daughter's betrothed (salt, tobacco, or more valuable objects) give her useful gifts to match, such as cooking pots, foodstuffs, cotton and so forth, so that the young wife will have enough to set up housekeeping and to keep her, in fact, until the next harvest. In tribes without the dowry system, the bride's mother and aunts provide her with the necessities.

Among other forms of marriage contract, the most frequent, after the bride price, consists in bestowing the bride and the exercise of a right prescribed by custom. The ceremony of bestowal is found among the Mossi of the Upper Volta and the Bamileke of the Cameroun. The girl may be given free to a benefactor, who is thereby thanked and repaid, or to a chief or to an important personage whose favor is being courted.

Except for these instances, the bestowal is not a free gift. The Bamileke require a bride price and the Mossi require the suitor to prove his devotion by all sorts of good offices, services, and by numerous gifts.

One Mossi, Tasre by name, told me one day how he had acquired two wives, Yembale and Koudtibo. His father was not wealthy and he had many sons to marry off; so he had given Tasre, at the age of thirteen, to the chief of Bisgen who took him on as a servant. Twelve years later the chief said to him, "I am pleased with you, and I am going to give you a wife. She is Yembale, whom I sent for two days ago." Tasre prostrated himself before the chief, delighted that he would be able to marry. With the help of the chief's other servants, he built a house, and two months later the marriage took place. Tasre's parents shaved the heads of the two young people, thereby signifying that their life was changing through their marriage.

Yembale was fifteen years old. She was docile and industrious, but not very robust. She lost her two first babies. The third was a girl, Nobila, who belonged by right to the chief of Bisgen because he had given Yembale. Nobila remained with her parents and helped her mother, but Tasre foresaw that when she became fifteen the chief would send for her in order to give her in marriage to another of his servants according to the custom. Yembale was not strong enough to do all the work in the house alone, to help with the sowing and the harvesting. And Tasre began the long negotiations to secure a second wife who would help her, care for her and serve her. He chose a good family, whose children were all strong and healthy. He helped cultivate their fields and repair the roofs of their houses.

After two years, Weddang, the head of the family, said to him: "You have treated me well, I am pleased with you. I shall treat you well also." This was the formula for saying: "I shall give you a wife."

Tasre redoubled his attentions, and three years later Weddang sent him a messenger who said: "My parents have need of a chicken and a goat in order to offer sacrifice to our ancestors."

Tasre then went to Weddang, taking with him the two animals requested. These were sacrificed before the whole family and eaten by them. Then Weddang said to Tasre: "Return to your home, and within seven days, children will come to greet you." And in seven days, Weddang's messengers presented themselves to the chief of Tasre's village and said: "Our father sends us to tell you that your son Tasre is a friend of our family, and he finds nothing to offer him. If he offers him money he will spend it and it will be finished; if he offers him the gift of a garment, it will wear out and then it will be finished. All that our father may offer him will disappear except a person. But he has a small thing [that is, a little girl] and he thinks of giving her to his friend so that she may draw water for him." All present, with Tasre in the lead, then began to dance for joy crying: "*Wobro! Wobro!*" (elephant). "He has given me a wife as big as an elephant."

Weddang's messengers returned home laden with gifts from Tasre: sheep, chickens, tobacco, millet, beer and many other articles. Soon afterward Tasre went to thank his father-in-law, who said to him: "I shall give you Koudtibo." Then Tasre prostrated himself in front of Weddang to thank him.

Koudibo was a pretty little girl eight years old. From then on she came every year to spend some time in Tasre's house. Yembale took care of her and Tasre gave her presents, which won her affection. But he still had to help his future parents-in-law throughout the seasons, spading, sowing, weeding and hoeing, and finally at harvest time. He also had to help them replaster (with clay) their houses after the rainy season and repair the thatch. Toward the last, when his future father-in-law fell ill Tasre cared for him and paid the tax for the whole family. For that he had to borrow from his brothers, and when I knew him he had just finished paying them back. Finally when Koudtibo was seventeen years old, the wedding date was set, but this time it was not necessary to shave his head for Koudtibo was not the first wife. On the appointed day, Koudtibo's parents brought her to her husband's village. She was received as an important person, all the relatives inviting her to stay with them. After several days the wedding feast took place. Tasre had killed a sheep, and there was a great dinner, with much millet beer. In the afternoon the young bride prepared Tasre's evening meal and served him, and that night she stayed with him.

The next day Koudtibo's parents returned home taking with them more gifts: chickens and millet beer. The jars of beer were new, and there was also a whole roast chicken. That meant that Tasre had found his bride a virgin and her parents were very proud as they returned to their village. If she had not been a virgin, they would have gone home carrying jars that were new but chipped, and the roast chicken would have been split open.

Tasre's case illustrates the two types of marriage among the Mossi; the first wife was given by a chief, the second by her parents. In both, the first daughter born of the union is called *pugh'siure,* and she belongs to whoever gave her mother in marriage, either the chief or her mother's parents.

This means that the chiefs always have a certain number of girls at their disposal whom they can bestow on their servants. Chiefs also receive girls as gifts, and a chief can always give to others those bestowed on him by his subordinates. But it would show a grave lack of respect for a man not to keep for himself a wife that a superior bestowed on him.

Today many of the Mossi chiefs are Christian and they favor the just freedom of women. When the little *pugh'siures* who belong to them according to custom come to them, they supervise their education or send them to school, for often there are no schools in their native village. When they are old enough to marry, these young girls are free to accept or reject the suitors who present themselves.

The gift of a wife is irrevocable. "We do not give our daughters twice," the Mossi say. Marriage then is practically indissoluble although the customary law does provide for cases of repudiation.

The Bamileke in the Cameroun, among whom marriage is contracted through the bride price payment, have a custom similar to that of the *pugh'siure* called *n'kap*. In principle this is reserved to the chiefs, who, like those of the Mossi, exercise the right of property over numerous young girls and give them in marriage to their servants without requiring any payment but reserving for themselves the ownership of all daughters born of them. This custom increases the number of girls at their disposal and maintains their power by enabling them to procure cheaply good servants of every rank who are desirous of marrying one of these girls and becoming thereby a client of the chief in the old Roman sense of the word. The custom recalls the right assumed by kings and feudal lords in the Middle Ages to control the marriages of their subjects or vassals.

In matriarchal families, the girl is given in marriage by the head of the maternal family, sometimes her mother's brother. In West Africa many matriarchal tribes have the bride price custom. In some matriarchal tribes, however, the marriage (which we would consider endogamous but which they do not, since they recognize only one line of descent) takes place quite simply through the exercise of a customary right. The young man's father declares to one of his sisters that he is taking, according to custom, a certain one of her daughters for his son. The girl's father, on the other hand, has nothing to say; all the arrangements are made without him. In matriarchal societies, the African disposes of his sister's daughters but not his own. The marriage, therefore, takes place between cross cousins when that is possible, and the matrimonial destiny of the couple is determined by the custom, to which all must submit.

When a father has provided a wife for his eldest son, he then looks out for the younger ones. If the eldest becomes a widower he must wait until all his brothers are married before he may take a second wife.

A man who has no sisters, or whose sisters have no daughters, asks a more fortunate friend to secure a wife for his son. In return he undertakes to provide, in case of necessity, a young girl for a member of his friend's family. In such marriages, the gifts offered by the fiancé are regulated by custom. Among the Bobo-Fing of Upper Volta, for example, the fiancé must give certain presents and cultivate a field of sesame for his mother-in-law. Then his friends carry off the girl but this is still not the marriage. She ordinarily goes back to her mother for a year or two before being brought definitely to her husband's home. Sometimes the marriage between cousins is accompanied by a dowry payment.

In matriarchal tribes in which cross cousins marry, it sometimes happens that a father cannot find a wife for his son. If he marries within the same tribe but outside the custom this gives rise to interminable palavers: the wife he takes was to have become the bride of one of her cousins, who consequently feels defrauded. If an accord is not reached between the two families, the affair winds up in the customary court.

Almost everywhere, then, the betrothal is arranged when the future bride is still very young, and from the time the contract is made, the future groom begins to discharge the obligations imposed by custom. When a girl has been promised before birth, the gifts and services begin as soon as she is born. A minimum of the obligations must be fulfilled by the groom or his family before the marriage can take place. The actual ceremonies, which vary from region to region, are sometimes very simple. In some, as among the Boussanse of Upper Volta, the bride goes along one evening to her husband's home. On occasion, she may precipitate a real battle between the young men and the young girls of a village. The latter try to defend their friend if she is being taken away by force (i.e., if she does not want the husband chosen for her, or they do not know which he is, which happens fairly often among the Marka of Mali). If her being carried off is foreseen and she is willing (as among the Bobo-Oule of Mali, for example), then there is only a mock struggle.

Most often, the girl is led to her husband's house by the women of her family and by her friends, according to the customs of each tribe. In the course of the ceremony the bride signifies her consent by tacit acceptance and by going through the prescribed ritual. For example, among the Serere of Senegal, the groom's mother pours a little millet or a bit of cotton on the head of the bride when she arrives at the groom's house. Among the Malinke (Mali and Guinea) as in several Togo tribes, wise recommendations are solemnly addressed to the bride. Among the Malinke and the Bambara of Mali, the bride is led in procession to the groom's house, accompanied by her friends carrying her trousseau.

Before this "taking of the bride to her husband's home" it is still legally possible to break the proposed union. Ancient customary law provided for this when the young girl's consent was necessary for the validity of the marriage. In other tribes, a girl who did not wish to marry the young man chosen for her enlisted the intervention of other relatives. If their influence convinced the clan chief, the betrothal was broken. Such instances seem to have been rare in former times and today the large size of the dowry makes it more difficult to break an engagement.

Among the Mossi, the husband "gives a house" to his bride and then calls her into his own. In the Cameroun, among the Ewondo, Bassa, and Bamileke, the future couple used to give their consent before the two assembled families in a ceremony that took place shortly before the marriage.

If the bride is unhappy about the marriage (which she is not free to refuse) she shows it in her attitude, when fear of incurring the curse of her family or even physical violence, such as isolation or being bound, have kept her from running away. For in customary law, a marriage is valid even when one of the couple (and most often the bride) does not wish to give consent. On the other hand, I have often attended marriage feasts that were very joyous occasions, even though the bride shed the tears expected of a good daughter on leaving her parental home.

Since the marriage does not give rise to an autonomous household, economically and socially independent of the great family clan, the groom is not "on his own" — an expression used in the tribes of the interior. Like the son in the families of ancient Rome[1] he is still subject to the authority of the head of his family in all important matters. Gradually he may have a house and fields independent of the family compound, but he must continue to help his parents and those of his wife. If he lives in the city and so cannot help with the farm work he must give them presents of money.

Marriage brings the greatest change in the life of the bride. She becomes a woman overnight. She is bound to respect and obey her husband and her parents-in-law, and to a certain degree she belongs also to her husband's family. If he dies she can be given in marriage to one of his relatives. But at the same time she must obey the directives which her own clan chief may give her either in person or through an intermediary, for she always remains an integral part of her own family. She returns to it often, either through affection for her mother, or to seek support and protection, or to obtain a favor (a child if she is sterile, or a cure, etc.) by having the elders offer sacrifice to the ancestors of her clan.

The bride's family (unless she has been given in marriage by a chief) retains the right to watch over the way her husband treats her. In some regions, the family exploits this right to obtain repeated gifts from the husband and even to take her back if he refuses to meet requirements he considers excessive and cannot satisfy. . . . But the wife's situation differs according to whether her husband is monogamous or polygamous, and in the latter case as to whether or not she is the first wife.

---

[1] In old Roman law a son who became a flamen of Jupiter and a daughter who became a Vestal Virgin were freed from parental authority. Later this applied also to consuls and prefects, and later still to bishops.

5. Polygamy and Monogamy

While the practice of polygamy generally characterizes most African society today, monogamy is mentioned in all African traditions. Legends recounting the origins of the different tribes invariably speak of a monogamous couple with many children, from whom all the members of the tribe trace their descent. There are echoes of this early respect for monogamy in some of the marriage customs still prevalent among polygamous peoples today. For example, the Mossi of the Upper Volta shave the heads of the newly married couple, but this ceremony is not performed when the husband takes a second wife. Among the Bassa of the Cameroun the ceremony of blessing a goat, which is then divided and eaten by those present, takes place only at the groom's first wedding. The Ewondo call every marriage after the first one *Aluk-Baa* — "added marriage" — and each additional wife is known as *Mininga-Baa* — "added wife."

Monogamy is held in high honor among the Tamberna of northern Togo and the Lobi and Bobo-Fing of Upper Volta. At the turn of the century monogamous couples with large families were not rare in West Africa. In those polygamous tribes which permitted women a certain amount of liberty, a first wife sometimes refused to accept a co-wife.

The idea of monogamous marriage seems also to mesh

with certain philosophical concepts among sub-Saharan Africans. In 1906, Pastor Spieth, a German missionary with a deep knowledge of the Ewe of Togo, wrote that the ideas the Ewes have of the conjugal relation between heaven and earth intimate a concept of monogamy. "In his pre-existence each man lived with one woman and it is of the greatest importance for his happiness to have in this world the wife to whom he was already bound in the beyond. Without question the first wife is accepted as the wife of his pre-existence. She alone is the legitimate wife, bestowed by God and the Mother of the spirits, and it is with her alone that he can live in peace and understanding."*

During a quarrel it often happens that a man insults a polygamous adversary by saying "I have only one wife and so I am not a voluptuary who hoards women in his house." Sometimes a second or third wife is called *dzidzanu,* thing of joy, or *dikalspiunu,* a young man's thing. In the interior of the Ewe country they say that the harvest of a polygamist is used up by his wives and children.

Polygamous families vary in size from those with from two to five wives, to the families of chiefs who may have from ten to twenty. Chiefs of greatest pre-eminence may have from sixty to one hundred or more wives.

The practice of polgamy grew through the centuries and its origins are to be found in the economic and social conditions in which the people lived.

In the inter-tribal wars the men were killed and their wives and children became the property of the conquerors. The chief kept a certain number for himself and bestowed the others on his warriors. Gradually polygamy thus became the rule among the most powerful chiefs.

---

* Spieth, Jakob, *Die Ewe-Stamme* (Berlin, 1906).

As for the mass of people generally, women nursed their babies for two years or longer because of the lack of proper supplementary baby food. Fearing that a pregnancy could endanger the life of the nursling they would have no intercourse with their husbands until the child could walk by itself and was weaned. The husbands meanwhile, not having the same reason for continence, took a second wife. The monogamous families mentioned above, however, did practice continence. In addition continence strictly observed before a hunt or a fishing expedition or before an athletic contest (wrestling or a pirogue race) was considered a means of attracting the favor of the protective divinities and ensuring success.

In the predominantly rural economy women often found the farm work, household chores, and long hours required to prepare the family food a heavy burden physically. Since the system of hired hands was unknown, a co-wife was the natural solution for extra help. I knew one African woman who had even earned and given her husband the dowry necessary for a second wife, a young girl whom she had chosen for him, so that she would have a maid to help her.

In certain old families of Dahomey, who were scrupulously observant of ancestral custom, monogamy was the rule until the husband reached sixty or over. He could then take a young wife to care for him and his first wife in their old age. Among the animists, this was the only situation in which a man was allowed to take a second wife. Many did not do so if daughters or devoted daughters-in-law were living in the vicinity.

The obligation binding on chiefs to offer all travelers food and shelter required a fairly large staff. Since the preparation of food was the duty of the women of the household, this became another practical reason to have several wives.

Ten years ago a notable of the Bobo-Dioula people of Upper Volta explained to me why he had taken a second wife. He had been married to Wenda for sixteen years and theirs was a marriage of love. He had been a civil servant posted to the Ivory Coast, where it was easy for Wenda to find maidservants. She had had six children, two of whom died in infancy. All her pregnancies had been difficult and her last child had almost cost her life. In 1946, political changes brought her husband back to Bobo-Dioulasso where his position required him to entertain a great deal. But here Wenda could not find a maidservant nor was there a young girl in her family or her husband's who could help her. She could have taken a "boy" but was unwilling to do so because her daughter was twelve years old and she did not wish to create any occasion for problems. The work was too much for her delicate health and so finally she said to her husband one day: "Take another wife and that way I shall have a helper." Her husband was not very taken with this solution although his Muslim faith permitted it. He tried again to find a paid helper but without success. In the end he gave in and married a fifteen year old girl, who was healthy, a good worker but illiterate.

"I see," I said. "African women must react differently from Europeans on this subject."

"Do not believe it, Sister," he said firmly. "It is my duty to satisfy both my wives and since I have taken a second wife Wenda is no longer the same. She feels that there is a difference now and she suffers from the whole situation even though she was the one who wanted it. She simply did not foresee what her own reactions would be. Her parents were monogamous and so were mine."

This type of customary polygamy recalls that of the patriarchs in the Old Testament and is quite different from the polygamy prompted by passion.

Even today the customary social structure leads some Africans to become polygamists. For example, when a polygamist dies his brother inherits his wives and children. If the former are still young he marries them. "Can I neglect the wives of my brother?" he reasons. And if the deceased has given a large bride price for them his heir would consider it a great loss not to marry them.

A young man who is unwilling to marry the girl his father has arranged for him according to custom often finds himself in a difficult position. If he refuses her, he hurts the girl who has been reserved for him and who for years has looked to him as her future husband. He hurts her family, which is often a highly respectable one and bound in close friendship to his own. He also deeply hurts his father by failing to appreciate his choice and the sacrifices he has made to pay the bridal dowry, sometimes a considerable sum, not to mention the usual gifts to the girl's family. During a discussion of this problem at an international student seminar at the University of Dakar a few years ago, a Muslim student declared: "If I wish to marry the girl I love, I must take a second wife because I cannot refuse the first one, who has been given to me by my father." This simple sentence contains a painful psychological drama which can be fully understood only with a knowledge of the ancient custom and of the solidarity of African family life.

If this is a painful and difficult situation for a Muslim, we may understand it is still more painful for a Christian, whose religion forbids polygamy and who finds himself saddled with a wife he does not love.

Large scale polygamy is practiced for the most part only by the great chiefs. There are several who number their wives in the hundreds but it should be remembered that they are not all consorts in the full sense of the term. Some are the widows of the previous chief, who were too old to remarry and who still live in their former houses and till their own plots of land. Others, called "little wives," are the small girls over whom custom gives him jurisdiction. They are either being brought up by his first wife or are little helpers to his other wives while waiting for him to decide their future, which he does by marrying them himself or by bestowing them on relatives, friends, or servants.

Contrary to popular belief, relatively few children are born to polygamous households of this size. Mogho-Naba Sanum, who ruled the Mossi at the end of the past century, had 500 wives but only twenty children, all daughters. Mogho-Naba Kom, who died in 1946, had 350 wives and a total of forty-two children. The celebrated sultan of Foumbam in the Cameroun, Ndjoya, had 147 children despite the fact that his wives at one time numbered 1200.

Polygamy represents a great social injustice, not only for the wives deprived of familial intimacy with their husband, but also for hundreds of young men who, because they are poor, are deprived of the sacred human right to found a family. They cannot find wives easily where large scale polygamy is practiced by the wealthy and when most of the young girls are already promised to rich men who are already married. Contrary to popular belief women do not outnumber men, particularly between the ages of fifteen and forty, that is, the marriageable years. Where women are more numerous in a specific area, a survey taken among the family chiefs has revealed that most of the young bachelors (between the ages of 18 and 40) have gone off to towns and cities in order to find work and earn enough money for a bride price.

Consequently if a chief has twenty or more wives, this often means that nineteen of his subjects have to be content with bachelorhood. And if the notables in the tribe also have several wives, it means that many more men are forced to wait until they are forty odd or more in the hope of inheriting the widow of a deceased brother. Often when I have asked a man of forty or older whether he was married, I have been told: "I do not yet have a wife, but my older brother is ill" (meaning — I hope to inherit one soon).

It is not at all difficult to surmise the other problems resulting from the fact that numerous bachelors live near the compound of a polygamist. In most regions a chief's wife convicted of adultery was formerly put to death together with her accomplice. Sometimes the chief would have the fidelity of his wives checked by a diviner, whose methods were reputed to be infallible. For example, all the wives had to look into a receptacle filled with water, at the bottom of which were certain ingredients the diviner claimed permitted him to distinguish the faithful from those who were not. The latter then had to denounce their accomplices before being put to death. Among the Mossi the guilty pair were beaten to death, or else a red hot jar was fastened over their heads. Among the Fon of Dahomey the culprits were buried up to the neck in holes dug side by side into which oil had been poured to attract the ants. To avoid an accusation that was often false, the poor wives bribed the diviner with any gift he demanded.

Africans with fewer wives also have recourse to a diviner if they doubt the fidelity of one of them. Some time ago a Malinke I knew quite well, who had in fact only one wife, became very jealous of her. Suspicion finally drove him to consult a diviner of great reputation, who sold the tormented husband a magic powder to take with him when he went hunting. If he killed any animal whatever while on the hunt, his wife was innocent. Fortunately he killed an elephant and so had incontrovertible proof of her fidelity, and she was thereby rehabilitated not only in his eyes but before the whole community.

In a polygamous household, the first wife has a very important role. She is the wife given by God and because of this she enjoys numerous prerogatives. In some regions it is she who offers the prescribed sacrifices at the sowing and harvest seasons. Among the Mossi she must pour a libation of water mixed with flour before the harvest is taken in. There is a pagan belief that her husband will die if the millet is stored before the first wife has poured this libation. In a chief's household it is the first wife who trains the little girls under his care and teaches them the custom. In all cases, the first wife is the intermediary between her husband and her co-wives, for it is she and not her husband who looks after them and directs their work. She has full authority over them, transmits their husband's orders to them and their requests to him. She can even keep them from being received by their common spouse.

In the Cameroun, one of my friends among the Bamileke told me that in his chiefdom several women had not seen their husband for as much as eight or ten years. He had over eighty wives and he often said to the first wife: "Tonight, such a one will come to me." She would pass on the order but inevitably arranged to be with the chief before the evening's invitee, who was then obliged to withdraw. This maneuver was used quite commonly and it is evident that the wives of a chief had to stay on good terms with the first wife if they wanted to avoid petty or unfair reprisals.

There have also been cases where wives who never had relations with their common spouse were deemed sterile and finally left him. Some later became Christian, married, and had healthy families.

Every wife has the duty to stay on good terms with her co-wives, to care for them when they are ill and to look after their children when necessary. Ordinarily, the children call all the wives of their father "mother" and in some regions there is great pity for a child who has only one mother. "If she is ill," they say, "who will give him to eat?"

I have known several families in which harmony reigned among four, five, and six wives. Their division of the work made it easier for each one to visit her mother often and meet with her girlhood friends or a lover. For if their husband is old, they are apt to seek male companionship elsewhere. When the several wives get along well together they will on occasion unite to prevent, if they can, the arrival of still another. I knew one man with four wives who decided to take a fifth, much younger than the others, who were reasonably afraid of being supplanted. "If you take another wife, we shall all leave you," they told him, and in the end he gave up the idea.

But jealousy can also rear its unlovely head in a polygamous family even where there is exterior or temporary harmony. This happens when one of the wives tries to monopolize the husband's favors for herself or her children, and the others react in self-defense.

In families of fifteen or twenty wives, there is often one besides the first wife who has a special and important role with particular duties. She is always intelligent, wise, entirely devoted to the husband and usually no longer young. She enjoys the husband's confidence, keeps his clothes, and prepares his meals if he has some reason to fear poisoning. Among the Mossi she is called the *doumde,* translated as "favorite."

I once had occasion to visit a Mossi canton chief who had about forty wives. He lived in one of the larger towns whose market was famous for its cloth. It was vacation time and another Sister and I had gone to buy material for school uniforms. But it was also the rainy season and the roads were badly rutted from the recent storms. Our bicycles sank up to the pedals in the mud, and we went to the chief to ask the loan of two horses, which he kindly granted.

A Mossi Christian named Emile was with us and I asked him to introduce us to the *doumde.* After we paid our respects to the chief and obtained his permission to enter the women's courtyard, Emile took us to the first wife, a robust, dynamic woman, with an amiable personality who seemed born to command. Then we visited the *doumde,* a distinguished old lady, with bright intelligent eyes, but wrinkled and quite toothless.

"She never leaves the compound," Emile told us. Then pointing to several trunks in her quarters, he added: "Those trunks contain the chief's robes; the *doumde* has charge of them. She is the one who washes them because the chief knows she will not put any magic powder in them to make him ill or to weaken his spirit. She is the one who brings him the water in which he washes too, and for the same reason. . . ."

After we had taken our leave I said to Emile: "I cannot believe that this very old lady is the 'favorite' of the chief."

"Sister," he declared, "I assure you that she is. She was the *doumde* of his father too."

Then I understood that this was a problem of translation, and that *doumde* and *favorite* did not mean exactly the same thing.

"In Europe when a king has a favorite she is young and beautiful," I told Emile. He opened his mouth in astonishment.

"The young women have all gone to market, Sister. If I had known you wanted to see them we should have gone to their quarters first."

"What exactly is a *doumde*, then?"

"The *doumde*," began Emile gravely, "is a woman in whom the chief has complete confidence. Often she is a widow of his father who has already shown affection for him since his boyhood; the one who took care of him when his own mother was away; who gave him peanuts and other goodies. Generally she is someone who has not had a son herself, or whose son has died. The chief takes her for his *doumde* because he knows that she will never poison him and she will warn him if the other wives plot against him. The woman we have just met was the *doumde* of the last chief, who died two years ago. All her own children are dead. This chief took her as his *doumde* because he is sure of her devotion."

"But, then, what function does the chief's mother have?" I asked.

"She is honored and respected by everybody. Her son gives her the 'small wives' as her maidservants — she is responsible for their training — and other servants to cultivate her fields; altogether she has a very pleasant life."

"But what does she do?"

101

"She supervises her fields and spins the cotton they produce. This earns her money for new clothes."

"But we did not meet the chief's mother today."

"She died before he became chief. You know our saying: 'A mother is a man's universe.' While she is alive, the chief occasionally seeks her advice. After her death he at times consults the *doumde,* at least in matters concerning the women. For other things, he consults his brothers or the other men of the family, never the women."

"And when the chief takes a new wife?"

"At first she is more favored than the others. Her turn to go to the chief for the night comes more often, and when another wife cannot come when chosen she takes her place. Later, she gets the same treatment as the others, when a new wife arrives."

"Are there not some clever women among these wives who could exert a real influence over their husband?"

"That might happen among ordinary people, but I have never seen it in the case of a chief. The first wife and the *doumde* would never let anyone supplant them. As for one of the other wives — if there are twenty of them, she spends only one night a month with her husband, or if there are many wives one night in every two or three months. How could she achieve any influence over him when she sees him so infrequently?"

"And during the daytime?"

"Oh, during the day they see the first wife, who supervises their work, but never the chief."

"I thought the night turn was more or less a regular thing."

"In principle it is; but the first wife always manages to see the chief more often than the others; and then if she wants to favor those who flatter her she gives them the turn

102

of one of the others, who is perhaps nursing her baby or who must skip her turn for some other reason."

"What of the man with only two or three wives?"

"When a man has two wives they take regular turns. If he has four or five he chooses each night, saying to one or the other after the evening meal: 'Go to sweep my house,' which means that she has been chosen for that night."

"Does she prepare his meals that day or the next?"

"Among some people, that is the arrangement. Among us, if a man has four or five wives, they each prepare some food; he tastes each dish and keeps for himself the one he likes best."

"What influence do the wives have over such a husband?"

"Well, if a woman is a hard worker, clever, and intelligent, she might acquire a little influence over her husband. But that is not a good thing because she might use it to downgrade the other wives, and this would make them fiercely jealous. In the past when this happened, it led once in a while to their plotting to poison the conniver. But most men are clever enough to be on their guard. They are careful to be the masters in the house. If a man favors one wife and is harsh with the others, he could be in danger of what they would do to him. They could, you see, make him ill. If he were dead, they think they would be free."

"And would they?"

"Oh you know very well, Sister," said Emile gravely, "that the women are never really free unless they are Christian."

Some may wonder if a polygamist can be converted to Christianity. It is possible. I have known several who had two or three wives and who, in order to become Christian, kept one and gave up the others. These returned to their own families and later married Christian husbands. This was in a region where there was a great popular movement toward Catholicism.

But more often, and especially where the majority are Muslim or animist, a polygamist desiring to become Christian must wait until he is on his deathbed to be baptized because of the great social obstacles he is unequal to overcoming. Some I have known numbered among their wives the daughter of a great chief. To send her away would be to commit a serious offense against him and to expose himself to reprisals. In other cases, the obstacle has simply been human passion.

Usually, a polygamist interested in Christianity will have his children baptized and instructed in the Christian religion. He himself will be a catechumen and declare his wish to die a Christian.

Still another problem is presented by the custom of inheriting widows, as I have noted. Some Christians do manage to solve it, as did Albert, a province chief and one of our best friends. When I first met him, he had succeeded his brother Sobarhende several years before, inheriting at the same time 150 wives. About half of these were his brother's consorts; the others were their father's widows, too old to remarry, or "small wives," that is, the little girls who belonged to the chief according to custom and whom he had the right to marry off as he willed.

Albert was a Christian, with a wife and two children, when Sobarhende died. He wished to remain monogamous and so allowed the widows to choose their own future. Most of them elected to become Christian in order to be free to accept or refuse another husband. Within three years they were all married. Only four or five chose to follow the custom and Albert had assigned them to the family chief, who married them to Sobarhende's cousins. The old widows remained in their own little houses as before and Albert saw that they were helped and taken care of when necessary. The "small wives" he sent to school. During vacations they went home to their own parents but if their mother was dead, Albert's own wife Odile took charge of them and taught them the customary chores of housekeeping and combing and spinning cotton.

Odile presided over Albert's courtyard with a gentle firmness and all the authority of the "first wife" of a great chief. She also had the prerogatives of the most beloved *doumde* and enjoyed certain rights that before had been the exclusive province of men. When Albert was away, he entrusted the household and all its keys to her, which was most revolutionary. His predecessors as well as all the other chiefs in the country entrusted the management of the household (including authority over the women) to one of their ministers or a trusted slave.

One day when I was visiting him, Albert interrupted the conversation to hand Odile an empty pack of cigarettes.

"I think you have smoked enough for today," she observed but took the pack and disappeared.

"I do smoke too much," he explained, "So I let Odile ration my cigarettes for me. That keeps my smoking down." Odile returned with two cigarettes in the pack and handed it to him. "The last two for today," she said.

I thought of the polygamous canton chief we had visited two weeks before, sitting outside the house of his first wife while she knelt on the threshold to hear what he had to say to her.

For a province chief, twenty-five years ago, monogamy

presented numerous problems. A great chief had to keep open house. Giving up the hundred or so women who were kept busy in Sobarhende's day pounding the millet and grinding the flour every day meant finding other ways of getting the work done. Albert had at first had the millet pounded by servants and later he bought hand-mills. The servants prepared the meals for the bachelors in the compound and the more important guests. Sometimes Albert sent gifts of food to friends to prove to them that men could cook as well as women. He also introduced truck gardens and persuaded his administrators to do the same. Now the vegetables grown in his province are sold in the markets within a radius of three hundred miles to the great benefit of the local farmers, who once had been quite poor.

There are now a number of Christian chiefs like Albert among the Mossi.

On the death of the canton chief mentioned above, his eldest son Alexander succeeded him. He was a medical auxiliary in the sleeping sickness control service. He too was a Christian and let the widows choose their own future. I visited him two or three years ago and found many changes since his father's time. The old wives of his father and grandfather still lived in the compound, however, and Alexander and his wife Suzanne looked after them.

Suzanne was upset that she had not known we were coming. Otherwise, she told us in some distress, she would have prepared a European dinner for us. As it was we had a fine meal of eggs and fried potatoes. Potatoes were one of the vegetables Albert had introduced.

"Potatoes are so convenient," Suzanne said. "It takes no time at all to fry them. Almost everyone grows them now."

I asked after the old *doumde* I had met so many years

before. "She died three months after my father-in-law," Suzanne recounted. "She was very grieved at his death and did not leave her house again. I brought her food every day and took care of her but she hardly ate at all. Death came gently to her, without suffering."

"How old was she?" I asked.

"We don't know exactly. Sixty-five perhaps, or seventy. They say she was born when the first Europeans came to Ouagadougou."

"And what happened to his first wife?"

"She is Alexander's mother. You will see her shortly. She has charge of the other widows who are still with us. Since everyone honors her as the chief's mother, she is not unhappy here. . . ."

Whether the marriage is monogamous or polygamous the African wife keeps the ownership of the property she brought to it. This may consist simply of clothing and a few cooking pots or it may include gold jewelry and cattle. The husband must give his wife a house and sometimes he furnishes her work tools, but each wife must provide food for herself and her children.

This general rule is applied differently in the various regions. In forest areas, the men clear the fields and the women do all the gardening, sometimes with the help of the older children or a young man of the family who is living with them at the time. In the savanna, the great polygamists assign a field to each wife, which she cultivates for herself and her own children. In monogamous families or where there are only two wives, the women do the farmwork with their husband, who gives out the rations for each day's meals. In general husbands try to be just and please their wives for, according to a Mossi proverb, "When she is well treated, the wife one loves forgets the road to her father's house."

The women also cultivate cotton, maize, millet for beer, and the ingredients for the stew. Whatever they earn from cotton, millet beer or vegetable oils they use for their own and their children's maintenance.

Everywhere the husband must show respect for his parents-in-law, help them according to his possibilities, offer generous hospitality when they visit him and pay for their trip home if this is necessary. When they die, he must bear his share of the funeral expenses, whatever they are. If he neglects his duties or mistreats his wife and she leaves his house, the husband who has only one or two wives and little money usually goes after the fugitive, bearing a gift of repentance. Unless his faults have been very grievous this is usually accepted.

But if the wife goes home to her parents without a reason sanctioned by the custom and without authorization or if she runs away, the husband demands her back from her father or whoever had the authority to give her to him. If she is not returned, he takes his case to the chief, who passes judgment according to customary law and orders the wife to return to her husband.

Formerly customary law did not sanction divorce except for very serious reasons, such as the husband's impotence, physical cruelty, mutilation of the wife, or a serious offense against the parents-in-law. Divorce was practically unknown in some tribes. In any case, divorce was not a legal but a family matter. If a wife was badly mistreated, her father took her home and a husband proved guilty had no right to reclaim her. If the wife's family took her back without good reason, they had to refund the bride price. In other words, the traditional African family, which has the right to arrange the marriages of its members, considers that it also has the right to dissolve them for reasons which it deems valid. This can of course give rise to serious abuse. Most often this occurs over money matters, but it can also be prompted by personal injuries and resentments.

I remember a young African doctor who divorced his wife after fifteen years of marriage. She was a mid-wife, of good family like his own, but she considered herself the equal of his brothers and cousins and refused to accept their superior and unkindly conduct toward her. Since she had no children, his brothers and cousins forced him to choose between them and her. He loved his wife and their life together was a happy one. They had jointly bought a piece of land and built a house on it. It was a marriage that could be expected to last. Yet the husband gave in to the pressures and threats of his brothers and asked for a divorce despite his wife's tears. She was no longer young and would find it difficult to re-marry, for none of her husband's friends would marry her while he was still alive.

"What happened to the house," I asked a mutual friend.

"They decided to sell it and divide the proceeds," I was told. "That proves they loved each other; otherwise the husband would have kept everything, and she would not have recovered a cent of what she put into it."

A husband always has the right to repudiate a wife found guilty of stealing or of adultery. In the latter case, the mildest forms of punishment were a necklace of red hot pieces of pottery or a vaginal douche of hot pepper. Often the guilty pair were put to death or sold into slavery.

But it was not permissible to divorce a wife because she

was sterile or no longer pleasing or too old or hard to get along with. If an African sent his wife away for one of these reasons, he would not find another to marry him.

If public rumor accused a woman of witchcraft or of being an "eater of souls," she was immediately repudiated and severely punished even when there was no real proof of her guilt. Divorce or repudiation, however, seems in the past to have been relatively rare. The African marriage was a stable one and some of the rites which still persist seem to indicate that in ancient custom it was considered indissoluble.

Among the Bassa of the Cameroun, for example, one may, in the capacity of spouse, partake only once of the food shared to consecrate the marriage. Among the Akebou of Togo the girl who accepts a mat offered by a young man is definitely betrothed to him and even if the engagement is later broken she cannot accept a second mat. Among the Boussanse of Upper Volta, a widow who has borne children (for whom, consequently, the bride price of four cows has been paid) cannot remarry legally because four cows may never be given for her a second time. If she becomes the wife of her husband's heir, this is nevertheless not considered a marriage in customary law and the children born of it are considered the children of the deceased. Even today among the Douala, a woman who has been divorced, whose bride price has been refunded and who has then remarried is not considered to have broken all bonds with her first husband. When he dies she returns to his house to mourn him and throughout the mourning period submits to all the rites prescribed for widows.

While the death of a wife dissolves the marriage bond, the death of the husband does not. In most tribes the widow or widows remain wives of the deceased until the ceremonies

110

that mark the end of the mourning period and establish that the deceased no longer has any rights over them. Among the Bobo-Fing, for example, the village smith breaks the bow of the deceased, saying to the widow: "From today all is finished between you and X. . . . You are no longer his wife."

In most tribes the widows are divided among the brothers and cousins of the deceased, sometimes among his sons. An African obviously cannot marry his own mother, but in the polygamous system it can happen that a man will inherit one of his father's wives who is younger than himself.

In many tribal systems a pagan widow cannot remarry outside the family of her deceased husband. She passively accepts the heir to whom she has been assigned without being able to indicate any preference. If she did indicate one it would cause suspicion that she had already had relations with that particular heir or even that she had caused her husband's death in order to marry him.

There are other regions where the widow has a certain latitude in that she may refuse to marry her husband's heir for a reason allowed by custom, for example, if the heir in question has a bad reputation. A Bobo-Fing widow says in such a case: "I will not put my hand in the mouth of a sleeping serpent."

Finally there are other tribes in which the widow may marry someone who is not a member of her deceased husband's family provided that her father or her new husband refunds the original dowry given for her.

In patriarchal tribes the children belong to their father's family and a widow who does not wish to leave her children behind her must therefore marry one of her husband's relatives whether she does so willingly or not. If she refuses, she runs the risk of great harassment. It makes no difference

111

in customary law if the heir already has a wife. When a widow is too old to remarry, the heir will keep her and make her help with the most difficult work. But if her sons are among the husband's heirs they will take care of her.

It is obvious that a man with many wives may love one or two at a time, and these may sooner or later be replaced in his affections. But he evidently cannot love them all equally well at the same time. If he is an older man, the young wives sometimes seek consolation in secret outside the conjugal circle.

In small polygamous households, if the husband has a favorite the other wives accept the situation provided he does not bother them and leaves them more or less free. But if a wife truly loves her husband and feels pushed aside for a new favorite she naturally suffers deeply. Often she will consult the diviner for a remedy intended to recover her husband's love for her.

If a polygamist treats all his wives equally, they get along well together, especially when theirs is a simple affection for their joint spouse, or if they are free to return when they wish to their own families where they have a "friend." But if he shows a marked preference for one of them, or even is tactless or thoughtless in his treatment of them, jealousy raises its disagreeable head among them. I once knew an African whose four wives were fiercely jealous of each other because he had given each of them headkerchiefs a month apart, that is, the fourth wife received hers three months after the first. And yet he had been careful to buy kerchiefs of the same quality and design.

If a woman was in love with someone else before her marriage, it may be difficult for her to love the husband her family has chosen and custom does not permit her to refuse.

"The heart is not a knee that can be bent," a common West African proverb says.

When the whole family dwells in one compound under the authority of the father or grandfather, the men live together and each woman, together with her children, forms a separate little family cell. In such cases, a close relationship between husband and wife is rather rare even when the marriage is monogamous. But if husband and wife have a separate home then their relationship is more of a partnership between them.

I once knew, among others, an old Bobo-Fing village chief who shared everything he received with his wife, even the official papers of the Administration, which she could not read. One day when he came to the Mission we offered him some cookies which he had never tasted before. He ate one, liked it and put another in his pocket. "I will give it to my wife," he said.

In former times, and to a great extent even today, most Africans live a simple village life. Everyone knows everyone else in the village; they all work hard and help one another as the occasions arise. Each has his own special role in the community and an influence commensurate with his dignity. Adults have the right to correct all the youngsters when necessary and all are bound by the same moral code.

In some areas boys over ten years of age may not spend the night in the house where there are women, but must sleep in quarters set aside for them in the village or neighborhood.

Almost everyone in a village is related to everyone else. It is believed that boys and girls cannot misbehave with one another without being severely punished by the ancestors, even if no one knows of their misconduct.

113

A natural morality based on religious beliefs is generally observed throughout traditional Africa, even though it too has its quota of malefactors like any other society. The great majority of Africans are good pagans who live a strict and simple life and who fear an inevitable misfortune if they violate the precepts of the ancestors, the prescriptions of the diviner, and the rules of moral conduct that are an integral part of their ancestral customs.

6. Religion and Superstition in African Life

African life and institutions had a deeply religious basis. For centuries African peoples have lived according to a religion, a philosophy, a wisdom and ethic inherited from the ancestors and similar in many ways to the beliefs and ethics of the peoples of our ancient history.

Sub-Saharan Africa was originally animist, and for the most part it still is. At the present time approximately thirty-two million of West Africa's sixty-four million inhabitants are animist, twenty-five million are Muslim and seven million are Christian. Of the latter about four and a half million are Roman Catholic and the rest Protestant of various denominations.

Africa's traditional religion, known as animism, bears marked vestiges of early revelation. First among these is the belief in the existence of one, personal, omniscient, and all-powerful God. His name varies with the languages of the tribes but they all know him. He is neither the firmament nor the sun but sometimes the same word is used to designate both God and the sun. If a man has wronged another,

115

the latter will be heard to say: "You have behaved badly with me; I leave you to him," pointing to the sun, or "I leave you with him who rises here and goes to rest there," indicating with a gesture the course of the sun's journey.

God created the world and men. Now it is he who creates the souls of infants and makes the plants and crops grow.

The story of the creation of the first man and woman is often very similar to the biblical account of Adam and Eve. Frequently it describes the creation of the tribal ancestors. For example, certain tribes of northern Togo recount that God created a man and a woman and placed them on the earth. The man was a hunter and the woman lived by gathering fruits. The man sought the woman but she fled him. One day he killed an antelope and set it over the fire to smoke it. The woman drew near and asked for a pinch of snuff. The man gave it to her and then offered her some of the roasted meat. After that she stayed with him and became his wife and they had many children.

Reminiscences of a far-off and much happier age which ended through an act of disobedience to God are found among all the tribes in one form or another. It is generally believed that at the beginning of the world the heavens were very close to earth and God lived among men; and this had many advantages. When one was hungry he had only to break off a part of the sky which immediately became a piece of meat or other food as one preferred. But one day the sky was offended and withdrew to the zenith, and since then misfortunes burden the earth.

There are several versions of the nature of this offense. The Samos say that one day a woman while pounding millet found the sky was in her way. She could not lift her pestle as high as she wanted and wearied with frustrated

116

effort she cried out: "You annoy me." Then she hit a great blow with her pestle against the sky and this rose up never to come down again.

According to the Gurunsi of northern Ghana it was forbidden to put ashes [for salt] in the stew if it was being prepared with a piece of sky, otherwise a grave misfortune would befall. One day a woman violated this injunction and from the moment that she dropped the ashes into the stew the heavens withdrew.

The Lobi have still a different version. It was forbidden to look into the pot while cooking a slice of sky. But one day a woman, driven by hunger and perhaps also by curiosity, peeked in before the cooking was done. Immediately the sky receded and men have not been able to reach it since.

The Mossi say it was forbidden to light a fire under the sky. But there was a leper whose hands were reduced to stumps and who could not cut off a piece for his meat. No one gave him anything to eat either and so he took his revenge by holding a torch against the heavens and these immediately rose up through the air.

Concepts of the divine attributes are rather vague in African thought. There is, however, a nebulous belief that nothing happens without God's permission. For instance, the Mossi say: "If God has not killed, the chief does not kill," meaning that if God does not wish a certain man to die all the chief's power will not suffice to take his life from him.

God is good. He loves men and takes care of them but he always does this, it seems, through intermediary spirits or the ancestors. God is feared, too, for if he can give life he can also take it away. He alone possesses life and might. He is the "Master of Might," a phrase common among numerous tribes. It is he who bestows life, health, material goods and numerous children. "The Master of distribution is God," the Mali Bambara say. Men depend on God for all they have, and they beseech him in prayers which they address sometimes to him directly and sometimes to the ancestors or spirits. Most Africans begin the day with a prayer that God will protect them and their families from ill fortune.

"May God keep me and let me become as old as the earth," is a common formula.

Greetings inspired by courtesy or affection often carry a reference to God and his powers. "May God heal you," one says to a sick person. To someone suffering from fever, "May God give you a cool body." Among the Samos of Upper Volta a wish for more strength is expressed by "May God put iron in your body." "May God go with you," is a common leave-taking.

Early in the morning a Bobo-Fing will say, "May God make the day pleasant for you," while at ten or eleven o'clock his greeting is, "May God make the sun kind to you," that is, not too hot, for in the dry season the temperature frequently rises to 104 degrees in the shade. Toward evening this becomes, "May God give you a cool night." And if one is working in the fields, he is greeted with "May God make your hoe fruitful."

God is frequently mentioned in the routine events of daily living also. A Mossi proverb says, "Nothing can harm the one whom God helps." And his providence for the poor is reflected in sayings like "God sifts the stones from the millet of the blind man," or "The orphan has stew to eat but it is God who adds the meat broth."

The Bambara of Mali express the same idea differently: "The toad has no tail but God fans him." And again: "While

God is in heaven the lion cub will not have to graze," that is, God will help him find meat. In Dahomey common expressions are "Man thinks, God acts" — "What God has done cannot be undone."

Since for the most part God acts through intermediaries — spirits, ancestors of the clan or one's immediate ancestors (a dead grandfather or grandmother) — an act of worship to God alone is rare. Where it does occur the animals sacrificed in his honor are always white. Most often the act of worship is rendered to God and the ancestors, or to God and the spirits, or simply to a particular guardian spirit. Among certain peoples (the Fon of Dahomey, the Dagari of Ghana and the Lobi of Upper Volta) one room in the house is reserved for ancestor worship and in it are kept their images — carved in wood or engraved on copper — together with the offerings made to them.

The priest of this natural religion is the head of the family, who pays honor to God and the ancestors both on his own behalf and for all its members. The rite consists of pouring a libation. This may be water mixed with flour, it may be beer — made from millet or maize — or it may be the local palm or banana wine. Along the coast it has become the custom to pour libations of whiskey or gin. Sometimes offerings of food are made to the spirits of the dead. But the highest form of worship is the sacrifice, offered in honor of the divinity, the ancestors or the spirits. Usually the sacrificial victim is a chicken or a guinea-hen, but sheep, goats, and occasionally oxen are also sacrificed. In exceptional circumstances in the past a human sacrifice was offered, the victim being either someone taken prisoner or a stranger passing through the village whose family no one knew.

Before sowing the crops many Africans sacrifice a chicken

to God saying: "O God accept this chicken and give me health; give health to my wives, my children and my servants. Help me so that my harvest will be abundant. Guard my strength and my life, and next year I shall come again to sacrifice a chicken." It is also common to offer a sacrifice or pour a libation to the guardian spirit of a field before gathering the harvest. Libations are poured before going hunting or fishing, while the favor of the guardian spirit of the family is similarly sought on the occasion of a birth, a marriage — so that there will be many children born of it — or for a cure. Certain tribes pour a libation of flour and water to God before offering the sacrifice to the spirits or the ancestors, beseeching him to come and drink and to permit the sacrifice itself. Sometimes a prayer is addressed to both God and the ancestors thus: "I have consulted the diviner who has told me to offer a white hen to my grandfather and my ancestors so that my child may recover his health. May God, then, accept this hen and give it to my ancestors so that they will cure my child."

A sacrifice of expiation or reparation, to obtain God's pardon for a moral offense or simply for a violation of a customary prohibition, requires the offering of a red rooster or a reddish brown goat or sheep.

In case of a public calamity, an important event or an urgent need affecting the whole clan or the village, there is a public sacrifice in which all the family chiefs participate. I had occasion to attend such a ceremony a few years ago in one of the larger villages of the Upper Volta.

It was the end of June and there was desperate need of rain. During the dry season, from the previous October to the end of May, not a drop of rain had fallen. Through June there had been a few brief scattered showers but not enough

120

to soften the ground so that it could be dug for the sowing. Without a real rainfall there would be no millet and this would mean famine throughout the region. The elders therefore had decided upon a public sacrifice to obtain rain.

About eight o'clock in the morning the drums began the summons to the place of sacrifice. When we arrived, about a dozen family chiefs were already seated, each holding a white chicken, but the sacrificer stood waiting for all to gather. The others came one by one, each carrying a sacrificial chicken and followed by his "first wife" bearing a pot of millet beer on her head. This she placed in the prescribed spot and then withdrew. The drum kept calling the laggards until about ten o'clock, when the sacrifice master took up his big drum and accompanied by two assistant drummers marched three times around the square.. Their drumming announced that the sacrifice was about to begin.

Since the sacrifice was being offered to obtain a millet crop three stalks of millet tied together had been placed on the two stones that formed the altar. The sacrificer took a chicken and cut its throat, saying, "O God, accept this chicken and give us abundant millet. . . ." Then he let a few drops of the blood fall on the stalks and the stones. He next plucked two or three feathers from it and laid them on the blood. Then he let go of the chicken which tottered and fell. If the victim falls on its back it is a good omen but if it falls forward or over on its side the sacrifice has not been accepted. On this occasion the chicken fell as it should. The sacrificer picked it up again and rising to his full height held it above the altar crying out in a high shrill tone: "Lilililili. . . ." The women — who sat apart from the place of sacrifice — rejoiced at the cry, for it told them God had accepted the sacrifice.

121

The same rite was performed with each of the chickens, one after the other, about twenty in all, with occasional variations in the formula — "O God, accept this chicken and give us abundant millet, give us more than we had last year"; or "Give us many children"; or "Give us more sons than daughters"; or again "Give us health" — depending on the family whose chicken was being sacrificed.

When this part of the ceremony was ended, the ritual master took up a bowl filled with millet flour and water and said: "O God, I offer you this flour water so that you will grant us abundant millet; we shall make food to offer you." Then he poured the contents of the bowl over the millet stalks and the altar stones. He next filled another bowl with millet beer and offered it in the same way, pouring part of it over the stalks and stones and drinking the rest. He alone has the right to drink what is left in the bowl, but afterward all the chiefs drink the beer brought in the jars. The chickens are divided between the sacrificer and the chiefs and eaten, and in this way they all partake of the sacrifice.

Africans believe in the existence of a soul and its life after death. A man has only one soul — which leaves the body only at death — yet he also has another self or spirit which leaves his body while he is asleep and then tells him what it has seen; this we call a dream. But this spirit-self is vulnerable while it is out of the body. It can be captured by a sorcerer or diviner, kept prisoner or sold among sorcerers in the "soul" market, or it may even be eaten. It may fall in a well, or if it wanders into a funeral it may get itself shut up in a tomb or grave. If it does not return, its owner falls ill and his relatives consult the diviner to learn what has happened to it. The diviner determines this exactly and prescribes what must be done to ensure its recovery. If, however, the soul has been eaten, the diviner tells them to make some trivial offering, such as placing a pile of pancakes or some eggs in the road. Then they understand that there is nothing to be done and the person will die.

When death occurs the soul goes to join the ancestors. For the journey it needs food, cowries to pay the ferryman across the river, to buy fire if it is cold, or to pay the toll if it is stopped along the way. Therefore cowries are placed in the tomb and offerings of food are made to the dead.

A body that has been laid out in a house for the prescribed time is often carried out not through the door but through an opening especially cut for the occasion in one of the walls. That is so the deceased will not be able to find his way back into the house to trouble the living, for it seems that, according to an African belief, it is more than the soul that survives. It is the very being of the deceased, which keeps in the after-life its individual characteristics and social functions, its virtues and faults and its susceptibilities.

There is a general belief that the funeral ceremonies influence the fate of the deceased. The Bobo-Fing of Upper Volta maintain that the dead cannot enter into *Wara,* their final abode, until after the *Sakon-kie* or great ceremonies which should take place every year but which now are often held every two years instead. During these ceremonies and feasts, which last several days, honor is paid to all who have died during the preceding year or years. The heirs are clothed in garments belonging to the deceased in a special ritual which frees them from every attachment to earth. Men wearing carved wooden masks represent the dead and in former times used to terrify the women and children especially since they had the right to strike them as they chose.

There are numerous Christians now among the Bobo-Fing, and they still hold the *Sakon-kie* as a means of honoring their beloved dead.

In our society, the dead are buried in a family tomb or a grave in the family plot. The same sentiment prompts Africans to guide the soul of the deceased back to the abode of the ancestors.

Several years ago in a Mali village I was surprised to hear the funeral drums since there had been no death. But a young man named Kire had died in Benena a few miles away and had been duly buried there. Now, however, his relatives were bringing "home" his soul. One of them, named Zoumanou, carried a stick over his shoulder from the end of which hung a chicken. Zoumanou could not turn around or look back under pain of death for the soul of Kire was following him. The procession included mourners and minstrels who sang the dead man's praises. It wound its way to the house of the ancestors of the village and all knew that Kire's soul had entered, for it was following the stick which Zoumanou carried in and set against the wall beside a row of similar wands that had already led other souls to the ancestral home.

When the deceased arrives at the abode of the dead, the ancestors welcome or reject him according to whether or not he has been a respectable member of the family. . . .

Most Africans believe in reward and punishment after death, for the abode of the dead has two divisions. Those who have fulfilled the tribal obligations gather in a cool retreat where there are beautiful trees and springs of fresh water, and where there is abundant food and delicious drinks.

The souls of the wicked — sorcerers, criminals, prisoners — are sent to a very hot place where there are no trees and there is never any cool relief. The water in a small lake is always warm and the souls, seated constantly in the sun, speak of nothing but their discomfort and unhappiness. "The sun is too hot! The sun is burning us!" they cry.

Among other tribes there is a belief that after death the soul is in the hands of God, who judges it according to its deeds. If it has done well God keeps it with him and it remains with the souls of its relatives. If the person has committed evil deeds then it goes "in the fire" for there is no purgatory. One sometimes hears an older man trying to stop a boys' fight threaten them with: "Stop hitting each other or else you will meet in the place where the earth is red and there is fire. . . ." If one does a good deed, he is mindful of a future reward. For instance, an African who shelters an orphan will say: "I take him in the name of God," and after that he treats him as his own child.

This concept of God as the rewarder for good and evil is the basis of African ethics. A certain action is bad because it brings misfortune; and this misfortune is due to the fact that God punishes in this world as well as the next. For God, who has created the world and human beings, has given them laws. He commands them to obey their parents and the chiefs and to respect them. He forbids stealing, lying, murder, hatred, making fun of others' misfortune, everything in short that is harmful to one's neighbor. "If you mock one who is weak you mock God," they say, "for he has made him that way. . . ."

God sees the misdeed even if there are no human witnesses. "Even if you go into the water to do evil, or you hide in a hole to do it, it will be known because God will

125

make it known," say the Mossi. In African eyes sickness, untimely death, unforeseen accidents are all forms of punishment for acts committed. As a result, a sick person will often make a public confession, spontaneously or at the request of the diviner, before the latter prescribes the sacrifice he must offer to obtain pardon and the remedy that will cure him.

In addition to the "bad thing" — which is always evil because it offends one's neighbor and indirectly God who forbids it — there are other things one does not do because they dishonor the family. Africans have a very strong sense of family honor, which is a powerful stimulus in educating the young and in maintaining one's dignity in all the circumstances of life.

Charity toward the poor is exercised for the most part toward members of the same tribe and it is usually generous. "It is the man with a hard heart whose millet is old," one proverb says. The hospitality which characterizes African life is also generous. The traveler is always sheltered and his needs provided for, even if one must deprive oneself or give one's guests food intended for one's own family. Gifts are always given with great tact even if the gift itself is not of great value.

"A fig given with respect is better than a kola given with contempt," is still another common saying.

Submission to Providence, resignation in suffering, courage in adversity and an exquisite sense of courtesy are all characteristic of the West African. The virtues of their traditional societies — respect for God and sacred things, for chiefs and old people, filial piety, patience, kindness, and a refinement of feeling — predisposed them to the Christian message.

126

For convinced and pious African converts generally, Christianity completes their beliefs and satisfies their deepest aspirations, the ardent desire manifest in all their religious practices; namely, to have a fuller life in more intimate communion with the life of God.

It should be recognized, however, that in many areas this religious awareness was considerably dimmed through the centuries where superstition, empty formalities and fetishism, layered over the natural religion of the Ancients, gradually stifled it, and the worship rendered God, creator and master of life, blurred into fetish cults and rites to appease guardian spirits.

Fetishism is not to be confused with animism or with the ancestor worship mentioned above. Rather it tends to replace animism and destroy its fundamental beliefs such as the omnipotence of God, the influence of Providence, veneration of the ancestors. Fetishism is the belief that the forces of nature can be controlled and that all human events — whether good or bad — can be brought on or prevented by certain magic practices which automatically set in motion the action of good or bad spirits having limited but specific powers. Certain of these spirits have charge over rivers, others over sacred lakes, while still others govern the thunder or the rainfall. There are spirits that preside over journeys or over activities like hunting and fishing. Still others are responsible for diseases. In one area, for instance, there is a spirit of small pox.

The spirits which are considered the most powerful are venerated — and feared — by a whole ethnic group, while others enjoy a limited cult in a particular clan or village. These spirits dwell in rivers or sacred trees, in jars and pots of every dimension, and in mounds built in their honor.

They are the fetishes, and worship and sacrifices are offered them.

Where fetishism prevails, the family chief, who was the priest and sacrificer in the traditional religion, has been supplanted by the fetish priests, who form a sect that extends well beyond the limits of the clan and sometimes beyond the national boundaries. By appealing to a fetish priest, everyone can acquire a fetish of his own, which may be a piece of any material at all to which the spirit attaches itself. This is kept in the house or placed in a field or by the side of the road, but it is necessary to know how to use it. Fetishism embodies no moral or ethical values. In its wake the moral sanctions implicit in the old familial religion disappear while fear of the punishments decreed by the fetish priests for violations they define make the latter seem much more grievous than moral guilt.

In clans which have preserved the traditional religion, children are taught by their father how to honor God and the ancestors and a very simple ceremony suffices to attach them to the spiritual entity which constitutes the clan in this world and the next. In certain Mali tribes, for instance, the father takes the boys and the mother the girls to the abode of the ancestors on a day appointed by an elder of the clan. This takes place when the children are from two to five years old, and during the ceremony they each receive a new name but they must never be called by it or this will cause their death.

In tribes which have adopted fetish worship, the cult is taught by the rulers of the sect and the training period may last from nine months to three years. During this time the adolescent boys and young men are separated from their families and gathered into special camps situated in the bush

128

or the forest. Certain tribes maintain similar camps for girls. If all are members of the same clan, they are taught the laws and customs of the tribe together with the cult of the fetish.

During this period of seclusion the initiates must at no time recall their former life and are supposed to forget all they have learned up to that time. The fetish is to become embodied in them, make them children again in a new life, give them a new education and a new name, and mark them with the scarifications which announce that they belong to this particular fetish and that it has absolute power over them and all their possessions.

The initiates learn the language of the fetish, the dances in its honor, the rules of the sect, and sometimes how to make poisons to punish with sickness or even death any who offend the fetish, violate its laws or reveal the secrets of the sect. Those so punished are said to be "killed by the fetish."

Sometimes in the course of the training one of the initiates disappears altogether. His parents are not informed until the ceremony marking the end of the period, when they are told, "The fetish did not make him a child again." They say nothing despite their grief because it is the fetish that has taken their child. Serpos Tidjani, describing this practice in Dahomey, writes thus: "It sometimes happens that certain ones are chosen by the god and remain forever in the realm of the shades. The favor of the gods makes its demands. Tears and condolences are strictly forbidden."*

Sometimes the fetish cult merges certain magic beliefs or superstitions current in a region. For example, some populations are convinced that there is a mysterious relationship between the life of members of their clan and that of

---

* From "Rituels" in *Présence Africaine,* March, 1950, p. 297.

a specific animal group. Some Gurunsi believe there is a parallel life between the crocodiles of a certain pond and the inhabitants of their village. For instance, when a woman gives birth to a child, a baby crocodile is born in the pond. When a crocodile dies, it is at the same moment that death takes one of the villagers. Consequently, it is forbidden to kill a crocodile since this would cause the death of a clan member. Sometimes it is the antelope or another bush animal whose life is bound to that of the members of a given tribe.

This type of belief, however, is not to be confused with the many legends that recount how a certain animal saved the life of a particular ancestor and how out of gratitude he commanded his children and all his descendants to respect that animal, never to do it harm, and never to eat its flesh even when it died a natural death. Anyone violating this command even involuntarily could suffer painful consequences, for the offended ancestor would punish the disobedience with sickness, an accident, or some other misfortune.

Thus happenings which are either normal or due to natural causes — like sickness, drowning, an accidental fall, a fire — are commonly attributed to some external cause, such as an ancestor's indignation, the vengeance of a fetish, an enemy's hatred, or a neighbor's envy.

To cure an illness, to remedy or limit the consequences of a misfortune or, better, to prevent it in the first place, one consults a diviner. He is one who can read secrets hidden in the entrails of a hen, in the direction a spider crawls, or in the way a handful of shells tossed in the air fall back on the ground. He can then indicate the cause, or the author, of the misfortune and the appropriate sacrifices to be offered. His wares include antidotes, cures, amulets against bad luck; talismans guaranteed to keep one strong and healthy (often a panther tooth worn about the neck, wrist, or ankle); objects that carry a spell to cause the death of an enemy when set in his path; charms (often roots or special grasses) to secure the love of a woman or the return of an unfaithful husband; millet stalks bound together with bark to keep away thieves; or better still a guardian fetish inhabited by a spirit or under its influence.

Many of the superstitions and magic practices which have been flourishing in Europe and Asia through the centuries have also found their way to Africa to compete with the indigenous variety, and the efficacy of some imported magic is frequently advertised in the local papers. The new magic, like the old, exploits the credulous with the easy promise of success with little work and less effort. But African tradition was more realistic: "For a good harvest, the best talisman is a calabash of sweat," says a Mossi proverb.

While the imported magic has been adopted to some extent by Muslims too, the latter remain faithful for the most part to the classic amulets of their faith — the hand of Fatima to ward off misfortune and the little leather bags, blessed by the marabout, which contain verses of the Koran.

Islam was introduced into sub-Saharan Africa in the eleventh century, chiefly among the more northern tribes. African Muslims observe the fast of Ramadan and contribute the prescribed tithe, or ten per cent of their annual income, which may be divided between maintenance of the mosques, assistance to the needy and personal charity. They also are faithful to the five obligatory prayers to be said each day. It is not uncommon to see a Muslim take advantage of a train or bus stop to spread his prayer rug on the platform

131

or beside the road, turn toward the east, touch his forehead to the ground and proceed to recite the prescribed verses of the Koran.

Among both Christians and Muslims, there are those whose faith, whether they were born or converted to it, is one of deep conviction, and there are also some whose convictions are less clear and who retain at the same time the old beliefs and fetish practices.

Islam accommodates more easily perhaps to local cults and ancient customs. While the Koran limits the number of legal wives to four, there are Muslim chiefs in good standing who have many more. Muslim observances have left intact the metaphysical foundation of ancient Africa, its philosophy of life, its desire to increase its life force, and its belief in one omniscient and all-powerful God.

In both Muslim and animist tribes, there is an abundance of proverbs and wise sayings that reflect the most conspicuous feature of African life, the sense of community with all that it implies — family solidarity, devotion to the clan, mutual help, a sense of justice and charity in all relationships. There are many of them, too, that are extremely reminiscent of the admonitions and proverbs of the Old Testament.

It takes common effort to accomplish a difficult task: "When they unite, the ants succeed in defeating the elephant." But sometimes it is difficult for people to work together. In that case, they are reminded: "If your neighbor has a cast in one eye, look at his good eye."

There are many proverbs to remind children of their duty to their parents and their imagery is usually vivid: "Your father has taken care of you until your teeth grew out; now take care of him for he has lost his teeth." Mothers need

132

help too: "The she-donkey has foaled so that her back may rest."

As for the training of children, the Bambara have their equivalent of "how the twig is bent the tree will grow." They say, "As you shape the brick in the morning, so will you find it dried in the evening." But as everyone knows, example is the best teacher of all: "The hind does not fear that her young will limp."

Other proverbs are reminders of the respect due to elders or chiefs, or contain the age-old universal rules for getting along in the world: "You cannot say in the presence of a live lion what you would say over his dead body." Likewise, "whether a chief is right or wrong he is always right." The proverbial unwilling horse becomes a dog in African proverb: "You can make a dog lie down but you cannot make him close his eyes."

Family background is important. If a man is brave and courageous, his son will be too: "The cub of an unarmed lion is better than the cub of a hyena that is armed."

Work is a necessity of life: "He who works in the sun, will eat in the shade." It also takes good will: "The man who gathers grasshoppers is not ashamed to bend." And it takes perseverance: "One does not dig a well in a day."

The equality of all men is a principle that must not be forgotten: "What has happened to the peasant will happen to the chief," even if he is rich and powerful, for "man lives with his wealth but dies without it."

It is best to lead an irreproachable life for "There is no true beauty with bad behavior."

What is inevitable must be accepted: "You cannot command the hunchback to stand straight."

It is evident, however, that people are treated differently:

133

"If you are fond of someone whose eyes are inflamed, you say that he has rubbed them with rouge; but if you do not like someone, his trousers are a sack. . . ."

On the other hand, it is good to watch one's words: "Your tongue is your lion; if you loose it, it will eat you!" In any case, one must always be courteous: "When you are astride an ox you don't speak ill of cattle."

Revenge must never be exacted from a member of one's tribe; on the contrary, "One must have pity on those suffering misfortune even if they once mistreated him" for "the remedy for shame is forgiveness."

"Life is man's marketplace; heaven is his home."

7. Modern Education and the Ancestral Culture

The African belief in God the Creator and the worship due him, the natural ethics that guided the moral conduct of pious African families — these harmonized easily with the teachings of Christianity. But with the Christian concept of marriage — monogamous and indissoluble — the adjustment was not without certain difficulties. The example of Christian families, monogamous in fact and by choice, aroused various reactions, from curiosity and criticism to sympathy and approbation. The right of free choice of one's spouse, the right of young girls to refuse a husband chosen for them, was particularly appealing. With new concepts of personal responsibility and freedom, Christianity made an impact on African family law first upon the Christians and gradually among their neighbors.

There were, of course, African family groups which already recognized the right of free consent in the choice of a marriage partner and for them there was no problem. But other African societies presented two main obstacles to this: the absolute authority of the family chief and the bridal dowry given the bride's parents. In the latter case parents could be tempted to ignore their daughter's wishes in order to keep the payment received.

This problem was not a new one for the Church. In medieval times, the Germanic tribes also required a bride price payment to the father of the bride. Since the Church required her free consent to the marriage, the custom was gradually modified so that the bride price was divided between the bride and her father, and eventually all of it was given to the bride. She was given thirteen pieces of silver (gold in the case of royalty) and a ring blessed during the ceremony. If she was a virgin she also received a *morgengabe* or "morning gift" proportionate to her husband's means. Eventually she received the entire "dowry," which often amounted to a considerable sum and permitted her to live comfortably in case of her husband's death. These customs eventually gave way to legal measures but they left a trace in the old ceremonial formulas. For instance, when Princess Margaret of England was wed, after the blessing of the ring, the bridegroom spoke the formula of 1662: "With this ring I thee wed, with my body I thee worship, and with all my worldly goods I thee endow."

Similar modifications have taken place in Africa during the centuries. Contact with the Muslim populations of North Africa brought African tribes near the Sahara certain customs not found elsewhere. Among these is the proof of the bride's virginity — the nuptial robe or a white sheep — sent to her mother the day after the wedding. If the bride is found to be not a virgin the groom sends a black sheep. Other examples are the custom of covering the bride's face with a veil while she is being led to her husband's home; the bride's "trousseau" woven or bought by her mother (garments, cooking pots, jewelry); the practice of exhibiting this trousseau to the appreciative wedding guests; the killing of a sheep for a feast to celebrate the birth of a child; the ceremony of shaving the infant's head and giving him a name on the seventh day after his birth; the custom of burying the dead in a white shroud.

European influence is more marked in countries along the coast of the Gulf of Guinea (Ghana, Togo, Dahomey, Nigeria) where the Portuguese, English, Dutch, Swiss, and Germans maintained trading posts or settlements from the sixteenth century onward. Those who married Africans duly paid the dowry to the bride's parents and gave her personal gifts besides, such as clothing or jewelry. Their children followed their example and as a result the nature of the bride price was modified.

Gifts now made to the bride include expensive cloths, embroidered robes, head kerchiefs, perfume, jewelry, and similar presents. They are placed in a basket of beautifully woven design, sometimes ornamented with leather and cowrie shells. Or they may be presented in a wooden chest with carvings on the lid and sides. This "box" belongs to the bride, its value depending on the groom's means, and is in addition to the customary gifts to her relatives and the bride price paid her parents. The custom prevails among the Nigerian Yoruba, in southern Togo, Dahomey, and Ghana.

Christians have kept these same customs, but for them freedom to accept or refuse the spouse chosen by one's family is mandatory. Where marriages have always been arranged by the family chiefs and a "good, obedient" girl always tacitly accepted the husband chosen by her father, this has been a decided innovation and has encountered inevitable difficulties.

137

Some years ago I asked a young Mali: "Does your tribe require the bride's consent for a marriage?"

"But, of course," he replied.

"And if she refuses what happens?"

"If she refuses . . . ?" It was clear he had not thought of that possibility.

"If she says no to the marriage, what do you do?" I repeated.

"If she says no," he echoed with some irritation, "we hit her until she says yes."

It is not uncommon in other areas also for a girl who has "disobeyed" to be severely punished, chiefly because her parents cannot understand the reasons for her refusal. The girls of the clan have always been submissive. The marriage is an honorable one and advantageous both for the girl and her family. The proposed groom is a notable, rich, respected by everyone. All his wives are treated well, they dress beautifully and he sends gifts of money regularly to their mothers. Why should she refuse to marry him just because he has other wives, or because he is close to sixty years old? Neither her parents nor her relatives can understand her attitude.

To make her accept they try first to reason with her: "You must say yes because your parents have said yes." If she still refuses she is threatened: "If you do not marry this man we shall drive you out of the house."

Her mother weeps and pleads: "I shall die of shame and grief."

Often in the end the girl gives in. But if she is strong-willed or has already promised to marry a young man whom she loves, she will resist all the pressures brought to bear on her. As a result she may be beaten, or she may be cursed

138

by the family chief who calls down upon her head the punishment of the ancestors. Sometimes she is brought by force to her husband's home.

It should be remembered that in traditional societies these marriages are arranged by the clan or family chief, who is often the grandfather or great uncle of the young girl in question. The two generations which separate them in Africa where changes are occurring so rapidly explain this complete and sometimes tragic lack of understanding.

When a girl has been promised by her own father, he may realize his choice is not particularly fortunate and regret the contract he has made. In that case the girl's mother intervenes: "Go to your husband," she tells the reluctant bride, "and in two or three months you may leave him. But then you will be leaving his house and our honor will be saved."

Some young women accept this proposition out of respect for their parents, even when they are aware of the troubles that may arise if the husband takes them to court and accuses them of "abandoning the conjugal domicile." Others, however, will have none of this solution, which they consider hypocritical, and prefer to go to court themselves to obtain their freedom.

One of the first to take such a revolutionary step was a young midwife named Mathilde, of Ouagadougou (Upper Volta). According to the custom she belonged to her maternal grandfather, Sandaorho, chief of a nearby village, because he had given her mother in marriage. The latter, however, together with her husband, Joseph by name, had become Christian and Mathilde attended the mission school. While studying for her midwifery certificate in Dakar she met and fell in love with a young Christian doctor.

But old Sandaorho regularly asked Joseph when Mathilde was coming home for he needed her. Joseph understood this meant he needed her for a marriage and was careful not to send for her.

When her studies were finished Mathilde came to her parents in Ouagadougou to wait for her assignment in the health service. Two days after her arrival Sandaorho appeared and congratulated Mathilde on her success. Then he added that he had promised her to one of his friends, a rich man and village chief like himself, who would make her a very good husband.

"Who is it?" Mathilde asked.

"Namkouma, the chief of Paspanga."

Mathilde gave a start. She remembered the old Namkouma. He had been failing and a leper when she left for Dakar three years before and he then had fifteen or sixteen wives.

"I will never go to his home!" she protested.

Sandaorho frowned. "We shall see," he said angrily and went off to the village.

Joseph was uneasy, for Sandaorho and Namkouma could send servants to carry Mathilde off by force.

Mathilde appealed to the district commissioner — since the country was then under French administration — who summoned Sandaorho and tried to explain why his granddaughter could not marry an old leper.

"I have promised. She will go to him!" Sandaorho insisted. "If she does not go of her own will she will go by force."

The commissioner saw he would not be convinced and tried threatening him. "If you take her off by force I shall put you in prison," he told him.

Sandaorho flew into a rage. "But this girl belongs to me,"

140

he shouted. "I have the right to give her to whomever I please.

"She has gone to school in Dakar and become a midwife. She has chosen to live by European law and she can choose her own husband."

Sandaorho was not convinced, but he was having other troubles with the administration and he did not want the commissioner to take too lively an interest in him.

"Very well," he grumbled. "Let her follow the custom of the Europeans." He left muttering a few customary maledictions. Six months later, Mathilde married her young doctor from Dakar.

Similar cases followed, and the decision was always in favor of the girl's freedom of choice. But French colonial policy was based on the principle of respect for the traditional African customs provided these did not conflict with public order. Something more was needed, a law that specifically recognized woman's freedom. A decree of June 15, 1939, called the Mandel decree after the Minister of Colonies who signed it, made the free consent of the spouses a necessary requirement for a valid marriage. It declared null all marriage contracts made for girls before the age of puberty and for those after that age if they did not give their consent, and finally it gave widows and all other persons who formed part of an inheritance according to custom the right to refuse to go to the heir to whom they were assigned.

In Ghana, then the Gold Coast, as well as in Nigeria the Criminal Code established by the British Administration in 1936 prescribed a two year prison sentence for "whoever by duress, causes any person to marry against his or her will" (art. 184).

However, many young women continued to be married

against their will especially in those areas where the bride price system prevailed. In early times this was something the average family could easily take care of. But the great changes in the African economy over the past thirty years have suggested to some a way to get rich quickly and without much effort. Where export crops are cultivated (coffee, cocoa) the dowry fluctuates with their market price and usually only the rich can secure brides.

Parents who take advantage of the situation reason that since they normally receive money in exchange for a daughter in marriage why should they not request more than before? If a girl's education costs more than in former years, because instead of helping with the work she goes to school, is it not reasonable to ask for a higher bride price? And if there are several suitors, why not accept the one who offers the most?

As a result the original purpose and significance of the bridal dowry gradually has been lost, its meaning in the marriage falsified and the girl's liberty entirely suppressed. Parents with a greedy purse have tried to get as much as possible from a daughter's suitor, while wealthy suitors invariably offered more to win over a rival. Where this happened marriage became a speculation and the girl a "merchandise" — to quote a member of the Camerounian legislature.

Before World War I, the standard bride price among the Bambara of Mali was about fifty dollars. By 1935 this varied between $100 and $200, in 1950 it had risen to $500 and over, while in June, 1958, an African official told me — with great indignation — of a trader from Bamako who the year before had betrothed his daughter for a bride price of $1,500. A few months later another suitor offered him

$2,000, so he broke the first engagement. The week before my conversation with the official, a planter from the Ivory Coast had offered this same father $3,400 and he had arranged to break the second engagement in favor of this third one. As for his daughter, she was barely fifteen years old and no one had thought to ask her view in the matter.

In the Cameroun in 1880 a chief offered with honor a bridal dowry consisting of 25 lumps of salt, two cloths, two pieces of flint and a pinch of gunpowder. At the beginning of World War I the bride price had risen to $100–$150 plus a ram and two hams for the bride's father and a goat for her mother. By 1932, the dowry for a widow (always less than that of a girl) was $100 plus a pig, two pounds of tobacco, a sack of salt and several calabashes of palm wine. In 1938 the bride price for a young girl was from $250 to $300, plus two goats, a pig, a great cloth, a large hat, a sack of salt, tobacco, and a large basin. By 1950, this had become $400 and ten goats, a cast iron pot and dresses for the girl's mother, a great cloth and other garments for her father, while by 1958 the sum varied from $1,000 in rural villages to $2,500 in the city. A frequent request is for $500 plus a new Dodge truck and two oxen; or for $2,000 and ten oxen.

These figures represent extreme abuses, but the basic evil in the present use of the system is quite general even when the bride price is not so high. For example, among the Ibos of Nigeria, a dowry of $600 to $1,000 is not uncommon for a girl who has been educated, while $300 may be asked for one who has not gone to school. To these sums must be added the customary gifts, which sometimes double the value of the bride price.

Where abuses exist the consequences are obvious: a kind

of marriage trade, with the girl's father, uncles, and brothers arranging all sorts of deals, promising her to several suitors at once and never returning any of the sums received, as it were, on account; increased polygamy among the rich, who are the only ones who can afford such exorbitant gifts, and enforced bachelorhood for young men of poor or modest means; abuse of parental authority on the part of greedy parents who oblige a daughter to marry against her will provided the bride price is satisfactory.

Despite these abuses, or rather because of them, some families now marry their daughters without asking any bride price at all or, at the most, for a symbolic gift that the suitor can present with little difficulty. They also give their daughter a sum equal to what they have received so that she will have all she needs in her new home.

With these families the custom is changing gradually and smoothly, and the influence of Christianity has contributed a great deal to the growing understanding of and respect for the girl's rights in the matter. In predominantly Christian areas young women have more freedom than elsewhere, while among non-Christians one often hears the pronouncement: "We no longer betroth our daughters when they are little, for if later they refuse the husband we have chosen, it will cause us much trouble."

There are still many girls, however, who acquiesce more or less willingly in their parents' choice of a husband. I know one young woman of sixteen who was quite happy to marry a notable sixty years old, although he already had several wives, because he was honored and respected by everyone and she had a great admiration for him.

Some girls, despite their personal preferences, yield to the pressure of relatives through fear of being excluded from the family if they resist. Just recently in Niger a fifteen-year-old schoolgirl, Aicha, had won a scholarship to secondary school and in all probability would have been able to go on to university studies. But her uncle had received a large dowry from a farmer, who already had a first wife, and Aicha permitted herself to be married to him. Her father was dead and she knew quite well that she could refuse the marriage. But her mother and uncles persuaded her that she was bound by the custom and the will of her family and she could not offend against either without bringing misfortune on herself and her children. She gave in, her husband took her to his village, and that was the end of her education.

There are others whose reactions are quite different. Recently another young woman, Potyilo, had begun her secondary school course on a scholarship. Her family, too, wished her to leave school to marry but she liked her studies, she was always first in her class, and she refused. She won her freedom to pursue her schooling by appealing to the district administration.

Where there is a well-organized social welfare service assistance is given to young women in winning the necessary freedom to marry according to their own wishes. The Christian missions are another source of help. When a girl has been betrothed to a polygamist whom she does not wish to marry at any price, it is often to a mission that she appeals for help.

The following letter received by a Father Theodore, an African priest, from a young girl in his parish in 1954 is typical of such cases.

"Dear Father," wrote the girl, whom I shall call Anna, "I must tell you of my trouble. When I was in school at Ebabod, a young man, Antoine . . . fell in love with me. We

145

became friends and he took me to his home to marry me. My parents came to claim the bride price and he gave them $60 and two goats. Papa thinks that is not enough. He always wanted to marry me to a rich man and when one came from Ngad (his name is Nnama) to ask for me he accepted right away. I refused. He came a second time and I refused. He came a third time and I still refused. Then Papa said to him: 'Keep bringing the money. The girl is still too young. She has the heart of a child. We will give her good advice and she will accept.'

"Every time my parents came to give me their advice, I answered: 'I will not marry that man.' Finally Papa said to me: 'Nnama has already given me many gifts. He will give me more and I will use the money to secure brides for your brothers. Go to him now; you are my daughter. Afterward we shall see what can be done.' I answered: 'I refuse to go; I do not want trouble later.'

"Nnama came again and said: 'If the girl does not love me, give me back all that I have paid you.' Papa asked me: 'What do you say?' I answered: 'I do not wish to go with this man to his home.' Then Papa grew angry and said to me: 'You have to go. You will go as surety for the things he has given me!' I answered: 'I told you from the beginning that I do not love this man!' Papa insisted I would go only as surety! But I said to him: 'I will go against my will. Remember it is a human being you are selling — not an animal!'

"I tried to run away but Papa caught me and tied me up and took me to the village. The chief of the village of Assila said to him: 'You must not send this girl to her marriage bound like that.' Then Papa untied me and made me go with Nnama. At first Nnama was kind to me. But when

146

Papa asked us to come and register the marriage I refused. Nnama took me home with him again and began to treat me like an animal. I was constantly watched. I took advantage of the market in Fonn to run away and I am asking help from the Mission."

Father Theodore immediately set about trying to free Anna, who was then hiding with one of her mother's sisters. He brought her to the mission where the Sisters kept her until the court gave its decision. The Cameroun was still a trust territory and Anna could appeal to the Mandel and Jacquinot decrees. The latter, promulgated in 1951, provided that a young woman could marry without her parents' consent when they asked an excessive bride price, the limit of which was fixed by the governor of the territory.

All Anna's countrymen who had some education knew why at the age of fifteen she did not wish to marry Nnama, who was fifty-four years old and had three wives: she would have been the fourth and the servant of the other three.

On the other hand, Nnama sensed that Anna with the help of Father Theodore could obtain her liberty. He did not want to lose all his investment so he appealed to the court of first instance for a refund of all he had given Anna's father.

The court decided that Anna's father should within two months repay Nnama all that he had received as an advance on the bride price, namely, $500, thirteen cloths (worth eight to ten dollars apiece) an aluminum pot, a bucket, two pair of shoes, two helmets, a deck chair, a pair of socks, a silk headkerchief, a large curved knife, two pair of gabardine trousers, one pair of black trousers and one of khaki, three shirts with long sleeves, eight gallons of wine, five chickens, and a book. These presents had a total value of about $400,

147

so that the amount paid on the bride price amounted to about $900. Anna's father was convinced that if he cursed and threatened his daughter with all sorts of misfortunes she would go back to Nnama and thus save him from reimbursing the old man since he knew Antoine did not have $900.

But he had underestimated the courage and tenacity of his daughter, supported by Father Theodore. The latter was anxious for Anna to get her freedom from her father's promise to Nnama first for herself and then for the example it would provide to others. Many other young Christian girls had like Anna been promised to polygamists. If she won her case, they would be encouraged to insist on their freedom.

The court then declared Anna could be free of the bond if she refunded the $900 that had been given for her. The decision was hardly fair since she had not received a cent, but the judges were all polygamists themselves and opposed to granting girls any liberty because, they said, this would be the ruination of parental authority.

Father Theodore advised Anna to appeal and she won to her side several influential Camerounians and Frenchmen who pressed the case both in the Cameroun and in Paris. The affair lasted over a year but finally the Court of Appeals decided she was free to marry the man of her choice — which was, after all in accord with the Jacquinot decree of 1951 — if he paid the bride price, which was set at $25.

Sometimes, however, out of respect for their parents, young women hesitate to go to court, resorting instead to other — sometimes rather dramatic — means to manifest their will.

In Yaounde in the Cameroun three young Catholic girls went so far as to make a razor cut across their throats to indicate they had no intention of marrying the husbands chosen for them. Their parents, frightened that they would really go ahead with suicide, consented to their marrying according to their choice and accepted the modest bride price offered. The girls still had their throats bandaged on their wedding day.

In the Republic of Mali the courts in recent years passed judgment on several cases of forced marriage. Among them was the case of a young woman who had been brought tightly bound to her husband's home. Her parents were condemned to several months in prison and the African Minister of the Interior took occasion to issue a proclamation stating that the Mandel and Jacquinot decrees of the previous French administration were still in force, and that any marriage performed against the will of the bride was invalid and constituted a violation of the law.

It takes more than a law, however, to change customs that are centuries old, and on occasion the local authorities feel they do not have sufficient power to protect a young woman even when the court has given her her freedom. A young Mossi girl from Ouagadaugau hanged herself twenty-four hours after she had been forced to marry against her will. She left a note saying she was doing this to claim for all African girls the freedom to choose their husbands. The case caused a sensation since suicides are rare in West Africa. Yet only a month later another young Mossi girl was forcibly taken by her father to the "husband" he had chosen despite a court decision granting her freedom and forbidding her parents to use force. The local authorities claimed that existing laws gave them no power to act, that at best they could only use threats which would in the end have no effect on the parents.

149

In traditional African society, following of the custom whereby the heir of the deceased married the latter's widow was often the best solution for her since it meant security both for her and her children. But with the changes taking place as a result of education and economic development, this custom has become extremely painful in many cases. Widows who have always lived in the city and find they must go to live in a bush village where there are no schools for their children and none of the amenities to which they themselves are accustomed find it extremely difficult. Christian widows cannot become wives of a polygamist.

I have known many women in West Africa, and in the Cameroun in particular, who were extremely unhappy because of this custom. If they refused to marry their husband's heir, their children were taken from them because in patriarchal tribes all children belong to the father's family. If the husband had given a high bride price his widow's situation was even more complicated. The heir insisted absolutely that she marry him: "Must I lose all that money, which was money belonging to my family?" As a consequence the courts often granted a widow her freedom only if the bridal dowry was refunded to her husband's family.

In this matter, too, there have been decrees and proclamations on the books since 1934, including the Mandel decree mentioned above, which in addition dispenses the widow from any indemnity to her deceased husband's family if she refuses to marry the heir.

But again old customs yield only with time to new laws. Often the same man will appeal to a new law when it suits his purpose, and on another occasion insist on the customary law if this gives him the advantage. One of my young Camerounian friends suffered from just such an experience.

Dorothy belonged to a family of civil servants. She had studied in France and her marriage to Daniel in 1950 had been arranged without dowry payment. Before leaving for France with her husband, Dorothy entrusted to her father-in-law, Victor, for safekeeping the total amount of her savings, the sum of $2,500. Unfortunately Daniel was killed in Paris in an auto accident just as Dorothy returned to the Cameroun to await the birth of her fourth child. Though she had not been brought up in the custom, she submitted to some of the practices imposed on widows — she cut her hair, wore coarse garments, covered herself with ashes and went to bathe in the Wouri.

Meanwhile, a Paris court awarded Dorothy $10,000 insurance damages because of the accident and an allowance for each of her children. Victor was convinced that the indemnity was due him for the death of his son. He began to harass Dorothy, insisting that she give him the money even though he still had the $2,500 she had left with him, and she understood quite well that he was after all she had. Two years after her husband's death she married a childhood friend, Bernard, who gave her great moral support and helped her raise the children.

At this, Victor instituted a suit against Dorothy on the grounds that she had not "respected the Douala custom by contracting a marriage without his consent" and without "having applied for her freedom as widow." He demanded the insurance money as his rightful inheritance from his son, and he also demanded that Dorothy leave her second husband and bring her four children to live with him. A first court decision gave Victor the custody of the children, but he was not satisfied. He wanted the money, too, and he appealed the decision as being contrary to Douala custom.

Dorothy, determined to keep her children and her second husband, engaged a French lawyer to prepare her brief but the hearing was a painful one for her. Victor stated his case thus: "In the Douala custom we know that the principal property a man has is the wife he has married. After the wife come the children, then all other property, goods and land. I do not understand why my property, my son's widow, is unwilling to share the other property with me when she herself is the chief inheritance due me."

Dorothy replied that her husband had been a student and had no property at all. She herself had lost the $2,500 and furniture she had left for safekeeping with her father-in-law when she went to France. But Victor would have none of this argument: "The widow is my property," he insisted. "How can she own property? All the property is mine, she has nothing. . . . A Douala woman must remain a widow in her husband's home and marry a member of his family."

When asked by the presiding judge: "Is it possible for a piece of property to elect representatives to the National Assembly?" Victor replied: "We have property that cannot speak and property that speaks. I could demand that the widow go back to the home of her deceased husband and that her second marriage be declared invalid."

The court in March of 1959 finally awarded Dorothy the custody of her children and recognized her second marriage, but in handing down the decision it declared: "Dorothy has treated the custom of her country too lightly in claiming her freedom as a widow." She was obliged to pay $400 damages to her father-in-law, for in the opinion of the court "while educated Camerounian women are not cattle to be bought they must however respect the customs, which have been established for their protection."

The decision might well have been questioned on the basis of the Mandel decree, but Dorothy paid the fine.

Fortunately most educated African widows have an easier time than Dorothy, who would have had far less trouble if it had not been for the insurance money. Most widows no longer accept the decisions of their husband's family and the case just cited established a useful precedent in most respects.

It should be remembered also that only the extreme cases are brought to court while the thousands of less thorny cases — those in which the widow gives in in the interests of her children — and thousands of instances of happy home life are not recorded in the daily papers.

As for rural areas, where only about five per cent of the girls attend school or where there are no schools at all, it never occurs to most young women that their lot could be different from that of their mothers and grandmothers and they adjust without difficulty — though not always without suffering — to the ancient custom. In the larger centers, three to five per cent of the women find their situation impossible and try to get out of it; about fifty per cent, despite their personal preferences, accept what they consider the inevitable, while about thirty per cent enjoy what is a normal freedom for the country within the framework of a sound and stable family life.

On the other hand, among the prostitutes in the cities are many who found their way there to escape family restraint or because their father or uncle demanded such an excessive bride price that it is taking years for their fiancé to earn it. Tired of waiting, they take to prostitution to earn money. Others left a husband they married against their will, and do not want to go home to their parents.

Sometimes a girl will begin to live with her fiancé once

he has begun to pay the bride price. But since the marriage is not yet registered civily — her father or family chief will not permit it to be until the whole amount is paid — their children belong to her family, i.e., to her father, uncle, or family chief, who can promise her daughters in marriage and start receiving a bride price for them. Most young women rebel against this situation. "Why have children, if they belong to someone else?" they say. "If we cannot marry whom we wish, better earn some money this way" (i.e., by prostitution).

All Africa's cities can tell similar stories, of varying degrees of tragedy. With education and when freedom of consent to marriage is assured, an end will be written to most of them.

African legislators are aware of the problems and are taking steps to solve them. In several of the countries, legislative committees have been set up to study appropriate measures. The proclamation of the Mali Minister of the Interior mentioned earlier declares that "any marriage contracted against the will of the bride is invalid and constitutes an infraction punishable by law." Several young women of Negala in Mali have as a result been able to have abrogated the betrothals contracted for them.

Recently, the administrator of Negala took occasion during one such case to declare to the crowd assembled in the court the following principles:

"A young woman is free to choose her husband. Only her father has the authority to give her in marriage, but he cannot do this without her consent nor before she has reached her seventeenth birthday.

"A betrothal may not be contracted before the girl is old enough to choose her husband; child betrothal is forbidden, and all speculation and bargainings relating to the bride price are also forbidden.

"A young woman may not be sent to live with her betrothed before the marriage, but after the marriage has taken place serious reasons and incontrovertible proof are necessary for a divorce."

In Bamako at a meeting attended by thousands of persons, including canton chiefs and Muslim chiefs, it was decided to limit the bride price to $150 for a girl and $75 for a woman who has already been married and to ban all other gifts. In case of divorce, this sum is to be refunded.

In Senegal the Muslim chiefs keep pressuring for a reasonable limit on the bride price so that young men of modest means may not be kept from marrying.

In Guinea, President Sekou Touré declared in September, 1959, his intention to free Guinean women from unjust restrictions and certain practices which are often humiliating "condemned by the women themselves and the source of physical and psychological suffering for them." The legal age of marriage has been set in Guinea at seventeen, the free consent of the bride is required and young women are urged to combat exploitation and the "indignity" which still marks their status in the family.

In the Ivory Coast there is a movement to do away entirely with the matriarchal system, all forms of bride price payment and forced marriage, and to ensure the naming of women representatives in all the economic, political, and social organizations of the young republic.

The Catholic Action Family Movement in the Ivory Coast has an extremely active program for promoting the status of women and freeing them from outmoded customs. At its national convention in February, 1959, it declared that "many ancestral customs relating to the matriarchate, the bride price and funerals no longer have any reason for existence in present-day society and hinder the moral and human development of the population at a time when the Ivory Coast is attaining its independence." The organization is dedicated to preserving all that is good in the traditional custom but to combating all that is contrary to human dignity and the progress of their country. The Catholic Action Family Movement, therefore, invites its members and friends not "to accept high bride price payments, to accept no bride price without the presence and consent of both parties to the betrothal," and to undertake a campaign among parents and friends, and especially family and village chiefs, to restore the dowry to the minimal value and purely symbolic significance it once had.

On the subject of funerals, surveys made in one region showed that often a sick person was neglected the better to do him honor at his death, when veritable feasts with considerable drinking were organized throughout the area. The Catholic Action Family Movement deplored these abuses and adopted the following resolutions:

1) that there be an educational campaign to create understanding on the part of relatives and friends that it is better to care for a sick person than to give him a spectacular funeral;

2) that the custom of drinking at funerals be abolished;

3) that not more than three cloths or covers be placed in the coffin, and that these be simple (as against the custom of placing several costly ones — ranging from $40 to $80 — over the body);

4) that all mistreatment of widows be abolished — ordeal by poison, sleeping with the husband's corpse, shaving the

head, smearing with ashes or other substances, tattooing; that she be allowed to keep her own garments (usually taken by the husband's family) and not be obliged to wear a coarse cloth and sleep on the bare ground;

5) that the widow's freedom on the death of her husband be ensured and that she be protected from attempts to deprive her of her own or her husband's property;

6) that the funeral ceremonies which take place long after the burial be gradually done away with;

7) that on the occasion of a funeral there be no colleclection of contributions (obligatory for all relatives however distant except in the case of needy families), that these gifts be used for the funeral expenses and anything left over be given to the widow and orphans;

8) that Christians substitute vigils of prayer and funeral Masses for the funeral ceremonies.

Other resolutions concerned the matriarchal system. This does not, as one might think, give woman a superior status in the family. It means that only kinship on the mother's side is recognized and that the men of her family have complete authority over her children. Their father has no rights over them and on his death his property is inherited by his sister's children, not by his own.

This custom "is rooted in legends without foundation," the Catholic Action Family Movement declared at its convention and it is "contrary to the true union between husband and wife and between parents and children." As a matter of fact the custom is not very much in favor at the present time among the people of the Ivory Coast.

A pamphlet written on the subject in 1948 by Monsignor Yago, now the Archbishop of Abidjan, led to the formation of an interdenominational organization (Muslins, animists, traditionalists, Catholics, and Protestants) to combat the custom. This organization — *Ligue pour la Promotion de la Femme Africaine* — declared that the matriarchal system is contrary to divine law (Gen. 2:24), the Gospel (Mt. 29:3 ff.), and the Epistles of St. Paul (Eph. 5:21, 28)

Legal measures, however, were necessary, since a young man wishing to escape from the matriarchal system could do so only by marrying a wife in a patriarchal family. Even then, he was still held responsible for his sister's children, and this inevitably led to endless complications in the case of his death or that of his sister.

Largely because of the efforts of Monsignor Yago — himself a member of a matriarchal tribe — the Catholic Action Family Movement and the above-mentioned *Ligue,* the chiefs and notables, at a meeting held in August, 1959, decided to abolish forced marriages, agreed that the right of consent of the bride, whether a young girl or a widow, should be a requisite for a valid marriage, and fixed the maximum bride price at $25 — plus a bottle of liquor.

On the subject of funeral ceremonies, the number of cloths to be placed in the coffin was not to exceed five, they decided, the slaughtering of oxen was to be forbidden, and the number of bottles of liquor was set at six.

Their most revolutionary decisions related to the matriarchal system, which was no longer to be recognized by custom. Inheritance according to the ancient custom was abolished, children were declared the legal heirs of their father, widows were granted the custody of their children and the usufruct of their husband's property.

These customary chiefs form an avant-garde in the progress of their country. Such modernization of the legal system follows upon the modifications of the custom gradually taking place in most regions of Africa, for education and the rapid transformations occurring in all phases of African society are bringing with them other concepts of life and freedom.

I recall a little Senegalese girl of eight or nine in a school in Dakar. The teacher had just finished reading a passage of African history, written by an African, which related how in former times when a king died several of his wives — who considered this an honor — were put to death to serve him in the next world. Immediately this youngster stood up, her long dress falling to her ankles, and asked: "Madame, when the wife dies do they kill the husband too?"

Evidently this young Muslim was convinced of the equality of the sexes and would be quite ready to fight for its recognition with the rest of her African sisters who are organizing to present their requests for appropriate legislation to the parliaments of their respective countries.

8. The African Child

It is often said that the child is king in Africa. It is true that he is at home in every house in the village, that every effort is made to prevent his tears, and when they come they are quickly dried. For children are the end and purpose of African marriage, awaited and desired by the wedded couple and both their families.

But in a region where the percentage of infant mortality is sometimes as high as sixty per cent, the birth and care of children is also fraught with anxiety and grief. I remember visiting a family of my good friends in a rural village to congratulate the mother on the birth of her fifth child. At the door I met her husband, Philip, and after the usual greetings and felicitations, I asked "And how many children does this make now?"

"Four," he answered.

"Four?" I repeated, somewhat puzzled. "But there are Jacques and Lucy at school, and Abel and Agnes here at home. . . . Doesn't Bernadette make five?"

"Oh, Sister, we do not count her yet. We do not know whether she will live."

Philip was an exemplary father, entirely devoted to his wife and children, and at the slighest symptom of illness he

160

always brought them to the Mission clinic. He himself had fortunately never suffered the loss of a child, but he had seen so many children die in infancy that his answer reflected the general reaction in the village. One did not count a child until it was certain to live.

In all West Africa, concern for the child's life begins before birth. Pre-natal clinics are a fairly recent innovation and unfortunately exist only in the larger centers. But the pregnant woman has always been protected in Africa according to the means at hand.

Among pagans, it was — and in some regions still is — the custom to consult the diviner, who advised the future mother on what foods to avoid, what persons not to visit, or perhaps not to receive visits from relatives nor go to market or other noisy places until after the child was born. Whether pagan or Christian, pregnant women avoid all food believed to be of possible harm to the unborn child. Among other things, very rich or fatty food, they believe, will make the child too large and the delivery difficult.

A Gurunsi woman (Northern Ghana) in her first pregnancy is supposed to be unaware of her condition until one of her husband's female relatives informs her of it by blowing a pinch of ashes in her face. The relative then takes the young mother's bracelets and necklaces to wear until the child is born, when she gives them back.

African women generally continue to do all their usual work, often very heavy work, right through pregnancy. Some claim that pounding millet and hoeing until the last day makes the delivery easier.

There are no special prescriptions for the husband during his wife's pregnancy, except that in some regions he must not engage in certain types of activity. For example, a

Gurunsi must not help to bury a dead person, for it is believed that the odor of the corpse will cling to him and cause a miscarriage.

In certain tribes the child's layette and the cloths in which the mother will carry him on her back are prepared ahead of time. In Northern Ghana and in Upper Volta an expectant mother weaves a charming wicker cradle shaped somewhat like a tray, in which she will carry her baby on her head. Everywhere mothers-to-be lay in great supplies of wood (the only fuel in many areas) and buy perfumed soap or make their own of shea butter or palm oil. If a mother has previously lost other babies, or in some regions even if she is expecting her first child, it is considered very dangerous to prepare a layette, for this will attract the attention of the evil spirits which are always prowling about. They may make the child ill or even cause his death, and so only old things and tattered cloths are set aside for the time of his birth.

In coastal towns, on the other hand, it is not unusual to see a woman set out for the maternity clinic carrying on her head a large enamel basin filled with the baby's layette, little bonnets and crocheted booties, talcum and toilet water, and anything else she thinks she or the baby will need.

In the interior, a woman generally gives birth at home, either under a lean-to attached to the house or in a hut built behind it just for this occasion. There she performs the traditional birth rites which are believed to have an influence on the health and even the life of the newborn infant. For this reason, women will often refuse to go to a maternity clinic newly established in the area and with which they are not yet familiar, because there it will not be possible to perform the ancestral rites. On several different occasions I have

162

known one or another young woman whose baby died of umbilical tetanus a few days after birth for lack of asepsis. When another child was on the way I would advise her to go to the government clinic a short two miles away and she would promise to do so. The older women in the family, however, invariably refused to permit any neglect of the ancestral customs and insisted she deliver at home. But a short two hours after the birth, she placed her baby in a calabash, the calabash on her head and off she walked the two miles to the clinic.

In bush villages, where there are no doctors or midwives and the local matrons have no notion of asepsis, a difficult delivery may mean the mother's death. A few hours after this happens, the village smith will open the mother and take out the child, who is then buried with her.

If the smith operates immediately upon the mother's death and the child is still alive when he removes it — or if the mother's death occurs after the child is born — its future depends on the tribe and the place. Even where attempt is made to keep him alive, this is difficult where there are no dispensaries or child care centers nearby, and where, in customary regions, no woman will consent to nurse him for fear that the vengeance of death will fall upon her own child. The tiny orphan usually dies within a few days unless his father takes him to the nearest dispensary (often at a distance of 20 to 80 miles), where it arrives in a state of exhaustion difficult to overcome.

Even before the introduction of nursing bottles, however, Africans exercised great ingenuity in feeding a child whose mother had died or was very ill. The Bambara of Mali, for example, used a squirrel skin, carefully sewn and filled with milk, the animal's tiny snout serving as a nipple.

163

In still other tribes, the infant was buried alive with its dead mother. In their view this is strictly a matter of collective security. The child which killed its mother as it was being born was not really a human being. It was an evil spirit that had entered the mother's body when she went to cut wood, or gather fruit in the bush. He is evil because his first act was to kill his mother; he will therefore kill all the other members of the family sooner or later and so must be gotten rid of at once. Christianity dispelled this belief, which is disappearing in non-Christian areas also with the development of education.

At his birth the infant is washed with warm water and soap and rubbed with shea butter or palm oil. He is then wrapped in a cloth and laid beside his mother. In maternity clinics, the infant's cradle is either beside the mother's bed or at the foot of it. If the birth has taken place at home a fire is kept burning for several days, and a relative takes care of the mother and baby. Neither one must go out of the house before the third day if the child is a boy, or the fourth if it is a girl.

Relatives and friends visit the mother to congratulate her and bring her gifts: combed cotton ready to be spun, ingredients recommended for the occasion, bracelets of woven grass, cloths for the baby, ornaments for the mother. Among pagan peoples, however, the visitor must not praise the baby, for this will bring bad fortune. She will say: "What a homely little face! What an ugly baby!" But then she will add: "May God grant him life. May he be spanked for his little brother" . . . a wish that the mother may have yet another child.

In Mali many young mothers wear a necklace of aromatic herbs so that the odor of milk, they say, will not bother them. Among the Bambara a young mother binds her fore-head with a narrow orange ribbon, which she wears for three months if the child is a boy and four if it is a girl. In still other tribes, young married women wear their hair like the unmarried girls until the birth of their first child, when they adopt the headdress of married women.

In some regions (the Mossi among them), the young mother goes home eight days after the baby's birth to have her own mother teach her how to care for him. She remains with her mother until the child can walk alone, coming home to her husband only twice a year for the customary feasts. Christian mothers, however, remain with their husbands.

Among many African people, the name given a child has great significance. In some tribes the father gives his baby a name that reflects his own sentiments at its birth. In others the grandmother, aunt, or clan chief names the child. In some areas of Northern Ghana, the child is not named until it is two years old. Then it is dedicated to an ancestor or to a guardian spirit of the family, whom the diviner has in-dicated wishes to be its protector and whose name is then given the child. Until this ceremony, it is called *Diampana*, meaning "without a name."

If in looks or mannerisms a child resembles a grandparent or an older brother or sister who has died, it is believed to embody the spirit of that particular person and so is given his name. If a child cries continually or is constantly rest-less this means that one of his deceased grandparents is dissatisfied. The diviner is then consulted to find out which one it is and the child is immediately given his name so that thus appeased the grandparent may restore its health. If the mother has made a pilgrimage to the tomb of a venerated

165

ancestor in order to have this child, the latter generally receives the ancestor's name. Among the Mossi it will simply be called *Yaorha* (tomb) to commemorate the pilgrimage. *Tangande* or *Bouri* is the name given a child whose mother has offered sacrifices to these particular spirits. Otherwise, a child's name may refer to some incident in the past history of the family or some circumstance of his own birth.

The name of an African priest of my acquaintance actually recalled a historical event that took place around 1896, in his grandfather's time, during one of the last raids of Samory's troops in Northern Ghana before the British occupation of the country. One morning this village awoke to the sound of galloping hoofs, the crack of muskets and the screams of men and women. It was a slave raid and the villagers fled in panic in all directions, seeking safety in the deepest recesses of the bush. Families were scattered and only the lucky ones could return after nightfall to count and bemoan their losses. One young woman had taken refuge in a tree, her baby half-sister on her shoulder, while her husband made for the bush, and the raiders swept through the village without noticing her. When her family re-gathered that night it found it had lost no less than eleven members. The old grandfather, or family chief, was heartbroken. He looked at the empty huts day after day and wondered how many would be standing when the rainy season came. Before the year was out, however, the young woman who had hidden in the tree gave birth to a son. The old man, on hearing the child was a boy, struck the great log on which he was sitting and exclaimed: *Atangba yire k an man lu,* that is, "the house that Atangba [his own father] built will never fall down." The boy's name, shortened to Akanlu, then meant in essence, "who would have thought that after all this disaster the family could survive, but here is a boy, in him it will stand." It was this boy who became the priest's father.

Among the Dagari, one finds names like *Yirwel,* the house is destroyed; *Don nuor,* the beginning of the war; *Mwon bare,* good fortune is ended; *Man nwor,* the riverbank; *Wa nye,* come and see; *Ti kone,* we weep; and many others. It is a region where formerly the population was decimated by sleeping sickness and so many common names suggest death. Among them one finds *Teng kun,* the country of death (and our country); *Kun ture,* death chooses (its victims); *Kun be viel,* death is not good; *Kun be fa,* death spares no one (here); *Yir kun,* the house of death; *Kun bar,* death has stopped killing us.

I also had a friend named "Elephant" because a stampede of elephants were ravaging his village when he was born. And one may meet on occasion an old man called "White Man" because his birth occurred when the first white men came to his particular country.

Some names refer in one way or another to God, invoking either his protection or his power. *Gmwin nong me,* for example, means God loves me; *Gmwin bie,* child of God; *gyre Gmwin,* look at God; *Gmwin be tuli,* God does not deceive; *Gmwin viel,* God is good.

The Mossi believe that women, whose work it is to give life, must never kill any animal. If a woman has accidentally killed a chicken, for instance, then to ward off evil she must give all her children the name *Noara* (chicken) or one of its variants — *Nobila, Noraogao* (for a boy), *Nopoko* (for a girl), and so forth.

Among the Ewe a child named *Kodjo* was born on Monday; if his name is *Kofi* he was born on a Friday. *Ablavi* is a girl born on Tuesday, and *Kosiwa* is one born on a Sunday. Among the Gurunsi, a child born the first day of the new moon is called *Atyana* (moon) if it is a boy, *Katyana* if it is a girl. *Awia* and *Kawia* are children born during the day, *Aduni* and *Kaduni* are names given children born during the planting season, *Abuga* and *Kabuga* denote children whose birth occurred while their mother was at the river to fetch water. *Ane* or *Kane* are babies who entered the world feet first. If one of the children in the family has recently died, the new baby is named *Apuri* if it is a boy, *Kapuri* if it is a girl. But not all Gurunsi names begin with A for boys or K for girls. I numbered among my friends three young Gurunsi girls whose names were *Awopole* (I am happy), *Abazang* (I am angry — but actually she was smiling all the time), *Amongo* (I am a mother), and *Meggra* (it does not matter).

"Names are given," an African told me, "to honor God's will, for it is he who has willed that the birth occur at that particular time or place, or in those particular circumstances." If the will of God is not acknowledged in the child's name, the pagans believe someone in the clan will die.

A sickly child is generally well cared for, and the other children are taught to respect him and help him if he is handicapped. A Mossi proverb declares that if you make fun of an invalid or cripple, you make fun of God, for he created him that way. Among some tribes, the child bears the name of his infirmity, such as "One-eye" or "Lame one," so that these words will not be insults to him when he grows up.

Twins receive a special name, and usually a diviner is consulted as to the choice. In some tribes a small altar is erected and sacrifices offered for their welfare.

If parents have suffered the loss of one or more children, they fear that the newborn infant may also be snatched from them by evil spirits. Almost everywhere various measures are taken to throw death off the scent. A woman may go to have her baby among friends belonging to another tribe so that the spirits that want to take the life of her child will not be able to find him. Or else one pretends to be indifferent or even unhappy about the birth and calls the baby "bad little thing," "sweepings," "shameless" or something equally uncomplimentary. Sometimes the infant is even laid on the dung heap, or it may be placed in a basket which one of the village women carries through the streets crying "pancakes for sale." All these devices are calculated to keep death from finding or wanting the child, whose parents ache to keep him and who surround him with every anxious care they know. Prayers are offered the ancestors, the diviner is consulted, and all his prescriptions are carried out to the letter.

In many areas, there is no special name-giving ceremony. Often, however, the child receives its name eight days after birth in the midst of family rejoicing intermingled with customary rites. Among the latter is the first cutting of the baby's hair. I was privileged to witness this in the family of some friends in Mali. The baby had been baptized Felicia in church, a name chosen by her father. But according to ancestral custom there remained the matter of cutting her hair. The house was full of guests — relatives, friends, and the one who was to perform the ceremony — all of whom had brought gifts. These consisted of millet, peanuts, combed cotton, kola nuts.

One of the women of the family held little Felicia on her lap while the ritual master snipped off her baby hair. As

169

fast as he did so this was gathered up by another woman and laid on a strip of raveled string. She had to be extremely careful not to let the wind carry the wisps of hair away, otherwise, according to local belief, Felicia would have a headache for a very long time. To carry out this custom her mother would have to keep her baby hair hidden until the child could walk by herself. Then Felicia would take the little package of hair and throw it into a deep hole, so that the wind would never be able to reach it.

When the hair cutting ceremony was over, the women presented their gifts to Felicia's mother, dancing about her and chanting their good wishes for the baby: "May God give her health. May he give her long life!" Next, one of the older women washed the baby with warm water and soap, using a small brush made of vegetable fibers. Next she warmed shea butter in her hands over the fire and rubbed the baby with it. Meanwhile, the guests were assembling for the meal, the men on one side, the women on the other, the old women in the house. The woman who had held Felicia throughout the ritual then set her on the back of one of the little girls and wrapped her in place with a long, new white cloth. The little girl so honored took her place among the other children, the woman joined the older members in the house, and the ceremony was over.

Christians have come to feel a spiritual relationship with the patron saint whose name they receive in baptism and with all others who bear the same name. In the various countries along the West African coast, it is not unusual to come across friendship groupings or associations of persons having the same name — Association of Jeans, of Germaines and the like.

One Christian told me that he had named his son Arsène.

When I asked him why, he replied: "I wanted to give a child to Father X . . . and this is *his* first name. This way he will have a son!"

Among the Mossi, a man may not bear the same name as his chief while the latter is alive. Each new chief changes his name on succeeding to power and he is never called again by his former name. All of his subjects who bear it are thenceforth called *Nab' Youre* which means "the name of the chief." But when a chief is Christian many of his Christian subjects name their children after him as a mark of respect, devotion, and spiritual kinship with him.

In former times each tribe had its own distinctive markings or scarifications. Thus a child kidnaped by an enemy tribe could always be recognized in later years, or fellow tribesmen could be recognized even in distant countries. In a way, these markings were also a guarantee of freedom, for no one, even the most powerful king, had the right to enslave a man or woman who bore the same tribal markings as himself.

These markings were generally made when the child was between one and two years old. Incisions — in the distinctive ethnic pattern — were made on the cheeks or forehead. Then a vegetable powder was rubbed into the wounds to delay the healing and make sure the scars would be permanent. When intertribal warfare ended, the custom of making these scarifications gradually disappeared, although certain families continued it longer than others. There are many Africans over thirty years of age who still bear these markings.

Child Care

No baby is prettier than a newborn African infant, with

171

his rosy brown skin, tight curly hair, and large dark eyes. Where water is plentiful his mother bathes him at least once, sometimes twice, a day and rubs him gently with palm or peanut oil or with shea butter. In the savanna, during the dry season when the water in the wells is muddy, she keeps him clean as best she can until the rains come and the daily bath can be resumed.

The African mother is in practically constant attendance on her child. In rural areas, he sleeps beside her at night and spends the day firmly set on her back. Whether she is pounding millet, walking to market, doing the family wash in the river, cleaning house or dancing at a family gathering, he rides in the snug security of the cloth that binds him to her and observes the world around him with an expression of round-eyed content. If his mother cannot keep him with her, it is an older sister who carries him in the same snug fashion. In the towns, however, cribs and cradles are coming into use.

Almost every African woman nurses her baby. If she works where she cannot take him with her, she leaves bottles prepared for the hours she is away and nurses him when she gets home. The minute he cries, he is fed, "demand feeding" being an old African custom.

Where tradition still prevails, it is believed necessary for the child's health to make him swallow some warm concoction every day. The mother brews a kind of tea of bitter herbs and then, seated on her mat, she holds the child firmly between her legs and makes him drink it all no matter how much he struggles. Then she holds him up by his feet and shakes him to lengthen him before putting him to sleep.

According to both European and African doctors, this treatment often causes a dilation of the stomach or gastric disturbances, and young mothers who have had some education no longer do it. But if they are living with their mothers or mothers-in-law, even temporarily, the latter insist on giving the child the same customary treatment and there is no way of preventing them.

I have seen this done many times and have said nothing since I knew it was useless to interfere in a custom to which the older women clung so tenaciously. But one day another Sister, who could no longer bear watching the little one's struggles and who was in any event a little tired of having her advice ignored, asked the child's mother: "Why do you insist on doing that? I am tall and strong, as you can see, and my mother did not do that to me!" A convincing argument, she thought.

"Oh," answered the child's mother, "you just don't remember because you were too little; but your mother most surely made you drink these things and that is why you are so healthy."

When a child is six or eight months old he is given porridge made with water and millet or corn flour, sometimes sweetened with sugar. But the porridge does not have the necessary nutritive value, and since his mother's milk is no longer sufficient either, this is the period when malnutrition sets in. Toddlers attempt to dip into the family dish at mealtime, but the stew of meat or fish is not the most appropriate food for them since it is highly spiced and often seasoned with an abundance of pepper which their little digestive system finds difficult to handle.

Lung infections are common ailments, while ignorance of contagion is another source of danger. To a grandmother with leprosy, for example, may be left the care of small children while both parents work in the fields.

Obviously there is a high rate of infant mortality — sometimes over 60 per cent — especially in areas where there are no clinics or hospitals. Half of the infant deaths occur before the age of six months, most of them due to umbilical tetanus or to respiratory or gastric infections. Later, besides the usual childhood diseases like measles and whooping cough there is danger from smallpox and the inevitable malaria. Lack of environmental sanitation and pure drinking water contribute a number of parasitic diseases, further aggravated by the occasional tendency of all children to eat dirt.

In areas where custom still prevails, when a child falls ill its mother consults the diviner. He prescribes the remedy, the sacrifice to be offered, and the amulet the child must wear to be cured. Some of the old remedies, handed down from time immemorial and consisting mainly of certain herb infusions, are quite effective.

If there is a dispensary in the area, a mother will not hesitate to walk several miles to bring her child for treatment. Unfortunately in the interior dispensaries and mother and child health centers are still much too few and far between.

It is customary for an African mother to nurse her baby until it is two and a half or three years old. The period of weaning is a critical one for the child's health and even his life. "Every adult African," an old doctor used to say, "is a survivor from the disaster of weaning."

The protein deficiency from which the child has already been suffering for lack of proper supplementary food now becomes even more acute, with consequent nutritional ailments such as kwashiorkor.

Maternal and child health centers, where they exist, strive

to combat these nutritional deficiencies. They teach mothers the elements of a balanced diet and how to prepare locally-available foods to achieve it. Where necessary the instruction given in the centers is followed by home visits. The need for a stronger network of such centers is obviously of great urgency, especially in the rural areas.

African children are very alert and learn early to observe all that they see as they are carried about on their mother's or sister's back. In addition, this constant, warm personal contact with someone who loves him gives the African child a sense of security that influences all his life.

As soon as he can walk, he begins to imitate his elders and, in rural areas, the whole village is his home, and there is no one in it who does not love him. He not only has the run of the village but is free to explore the world of nature about him. He is rarely punished and in case of danger refuge is always near in the person of his mother or a solicitous relative. This secure and happy childhood perhaps explains the warm optimism and joy of living that are so characteristic of the African.

The filial devotion the African retains for his mother all his life is abundantly reflected in the works of poets of French-speaking Africa.

"O Mother," writes Leopold Senghor, President of the Republic of Senegal, "they write that you are growing pale as the bush in the season of rains. . . .

"I would be, O Mother, the flowering palm of your old age;

"I would restore to you the intoxication of your youth. . . ."

And the Guinean poet, Camara Laye, in a poem addressed to his mother, whom he apostrophizes as "African Woman," reveals touchingly this filial devotion. He reviews

175

his mother's loving care of him in his childhood, her patience, her simple but memorable lessons, and closes his verse by thanking her for all she has been to him, her son "so far away, so close" by her side.

9. Education

"A numbskull is formed in the bones," states an African proverb. In other words, the first education a child receives is the most important.

In Africa the mother is the child's first educator, who teaches him his manners and proper behavior. Where traditional custom still prevails, his older brothers and sisters also undertake to teach him to obey them and to render them little services, so that he will recognize and respect their seniority. For example, at mealtime the youngest must never help himself before his elders and his hand must never touch theirs in the family dish. He must eat with his right hand and in silence.

Normally a child is not allowed alone outside the family circle until he is about five or six years old. Then he has the run of the village and takes refuge with one or another relative when parental punishment threatens. And like grandparents everywhere, those of the African child tend to spoil him.

Childish forays into lying or stealing, or any show of disrespect are quickly punished. The child may be deprived of a goodie, or spanked, or the punishment may take a more drastic form. For instance, a few years ago a Douala child who was given to stealing food was covered with banana

177

leaves and led through the village by a relative, crying, "Come and see the little thief." It cured him of stealing.

Girls have dolls fashioned of wood or a cornstalk, which in imitation of their mothers, they fasten on their backs until they are old enough to carry a little brother or sister. Boys chase birds with a branch, run after rats or lizards, or catch them in traps they have made themselves. In the savanna, millet stalks are easily transformed by their agile fingers into rifles, telescopes, locomotives, autos, or airplanes. Wrestling is a favorite pastime. They will pull each other around on palm leaves, play blindman's buff, and on occasion checkers.

Both boys and girls are athletic, and can shinny up trees or scale any rocky slope with remarkable agility. If they live in villages near a lake or river, they learn to swim almost as soon as they can walk.

When a boy is six or seven years old, his father begins to take over his education. He takes him to help in the fields, and when he is a little older begins to teach him both his own trade and the customary tasks about the house and compound.

The African father has a rich supply of proverbs to help mold his son's character. For example, "If the bricks say to each other, I will not stay next to you, the house will never be built." In other words, people must work together for there are many things a person working alone cannot accomplish.

Crafts, such as ironwork, jewelry making, tanning, saddlery, cordwaining, shoemaking, are passed on from father to son. The healer, or medicine man, will choose a son to succeed him, teaching him the qualities of medicinal plants and how to prepare his remedies.

The African girl remains with her mother until her own marriage unless she is being brought up in the family of her future husband. In either case she is taught how to keep house and cook, and she performs a number of errands such as fetching water and wood, in addition to helping take care of her little brothers and sisters. She takes the role of "little mother" very seriously and her care of a younger child is always affectionate. She also learns to grow the ingredients for the stew, to cultivate cotton and to comb and spin it. When she is a little older she helps to brew millet or banana beer and is taught how to make soap, weave mats or make pottery.

African women delight in decorating their calabashes with designs of their own invention. In certain tribes they also decorate the walls of the house and their everyday utensils with pretty patterns and create the attractive color combinaions in their basketwork. While small girls in traditional areas still learn these arts, in the larger cities most household utensils now are of European make and are bought in the market.

The mother is responsible also for the moral training of her daughter. Girls are taught to watch their tongues. "Your word," they are told, "is like a straw in the thatch. Once you have pulled it out you cannot put it back." Above all, one must not speak ill of others, for we all have our faults. "A millet stalk must not slander the other stalks for they all have bumps on them."

African girls also learn much from the examples of courage, endurance, maternal devotion, and resignation in adversity which their mothers frequently offer them. A girl's friendships are supervised for it is an honor if she is a virgin when she marries. "Do not trust a fancy talker," she is counseled, "and keep your dignity. Remember that when one acts like a goat, the hyena eats him."

The traditional training has a religious basis: fear of God and respect for the ancestors is an integral part of it. Here again example is the first teacher, for in religious pagan families children see their father offer prayers at dawn and at sunset, they assist at the sacrifices offered for the family and on certain occasions for the village. If by chance discord arises among the members of the same clan, it is the rule in some regions for the family chiefs to gather and perform specific rites and incantations designed to drive out the evil spirit, the cause of all the trouble, and to restore harmony to the clan. In several tribes, the father or grandfather gives his blessing to the children every evening.

This practical type of religious training, integrated as it is in everyday life, teaches the child respect, obedience, and other natural virtues, such as compassion toward the poor and the unfortunate and the habit of mutual assistance. A mother who gives food to a needy person will tell her children that "the compassionate man is preferable to a rich one."

Important events in everyday life are also used to teach a lesson. Prosperity is a recompense bestowed by God on those who are good and charitable: "He who gives to the Master of Heaven does not give in vain," is a proverb heard in Dahomey. One must be generous to the poor who seek help in the name of God; for, according to a Bambara proverb, "If you refuse God salt, he will refuse you fish" (i.e. you will have no success in fishing nor in any other enterprise). On the other hand, misfortune and reverses are believed to be a punishment for grave injustices or hidden sins committed either by the person himself or by his parents. When these things occur, a father or mother will say: "Our ancestors were right when they said, 'The evil sown by a great personage grows on the head of his child.'"

As the boys get older they take the evening meal with their father. Later when they are gathered in the courtyard in the bright moonlight he will tell them the history of the clan and the more interesting exploits of their ancestors. In traditional societies, the girls learn from their mothers to respect the family taboos. They do not assist at public sacrifices, but in certain tribes each woman has her household gods and associates her daughters with her in the worship she offers them.

The sense of family solidarity plays a great role in African education: "The ugliest man in the village must be esteemed more than the most handsome and richest stranger." In many traditional villages, all the inhabitants are more or less related. This solidarity means that each one has an obligation to help the others in every circumstance. And he also has the right to be aided in turn. To fail this family duty is an unpardonable injury. "If your relative has disdained you," says one proverb, "may he be deprived of you."

Family honor is a sentiment deeply rooted in the African heart. Parents inculcate it in their children, who accept any sacrifice to bring honor to the clan, while at the same time they will adopt all the hatreds and resentments of their relatives to avenge the family honor. Often when youngsters take to pummeling each other during a recess period at school, their explanation is that one has insulted the other's mother. This may be true, but if they belong to different clans it is not necessary to seek further for a reason.

Christianity has brought to this closed solidarity the concept of love of neighbor in the broader, universal sense.

The strong sense of family solidarity has opened to the brotherhood of all men as children of God, and the mutual aid which is the duty and right of every member of the clan has become the duty of charity to all inhabitants of the region whether relatives or strangers. This difference is most conspicuous in the youth movements, in which members of different and even once hostile tribes consider themselves brothers, help one another and when necessary are ready to make sacrifices for one another.

African parents favor all that contributes to the sound training of their children for they wish them to do honor to the family. "Even if a person has only one tooth, let it at least be white," still another proverb observes. An African whose son commits evil actions is considered the most unfortunate of men. For instance, there is a saying among the Yoruba of Nigeria that "it is not the father who has led his beloved son to the burial ground who needs pity, but rather the father whose son is a ruffian."

It is a mistake, however, to generalize on this subject as on any other. Parents too are very much alike the world over. I have African friends who make their children obey without lifting their voices, simply with a look, a gesture, a smile. But I know other African mothers who give in to every whim and later bemoan the fact that they have no control over their wayward children.

In rural traditional societies, a child's education is completed by a certain period of initiation. In some areas this applies only to the boys, in others it applies to the girls as well. Not all tribes have had the custom of initiation, and it has disappeared in those areas which have had long contact with government and mission schools.

In the interior, the initiation may be accompanied by

circumcision or excision, but the two are not necessarily correlative. There are tribes in which the boys are not circumcised during the period of initiation, but femal circumcision (or excision) is practiced. In others there is the practice of circumcision but no period of initiation.

Where the custom of initiation is still maintained (in a few limited areas) there are special camps for boys and girls. Sometimes the initiation for both takes place at the same time, sometimes at different times. Formerly it lasted several years, but now the period usually is limited to five or six months, though there are examples of eighteen month initiation courses. Isolated from the rest of the world during this period and under the exclusive jurisdiction of the initiation authorities, the youngsters are given a religious-social training in accordance with the ancestral beliefs and organization of the tribe.

In the course of secret rites — as in the case of the fetish initiations with which, however, these are not to be confused — the divinity, or guardian spirit of the tribe is believed to make each subject a child again in order to attach him to the spiritual entity which constitutes the tribe both in this world and the world beyond. The *initiandi* are believed in the process to forget all they have learned thus far, and so must be re-educated and learn a language understood only by the other initiates, in order that they may become men and women worthy of the tribe and of the ancestors. The initiation chiefs frighten the youngsters, persuading them that they risk great dangers and must blindly obey in all things under pain of incurring the wrath of the tribal genie. This acute sense of fear is sustained by means of a number of tests: difficult tasks, trials of endurance, rigid discipline, and severe punishments for the least infraction, together with meetings held at night while sinister noises fill the pitch black darkness. During this period also, the youngsters receive the tribal scarifications.

They are given a psychological and physiological preparation for married life which they will soon enter. Certain magic rites are performed to make the future unions happy ones, since most of the young women will be led to the home of their husbands soon after they emerge from the initiation.

In some tribes girls are treated as children until the initiation period. They can therefore say anything that comes into their heads and be as wayward and prankish as they please without being punished. But after the initiation they are women. They must watch their words and actions and behave with decorum and dignity. Any foolishness or misdemeanor on their part is then considered a serious matter and severely punished.

The end of the initiation period is the occasion for picturesque celebrations that last several days. The initiated don a special costume, dance energetically to the accompaniment of lively songs, and make a tour of the village to be admired before finally settling back within their own families.

As in the case of the fetish initiations, a child sometimes fails to emerge from the camp and the explanation is that the "spirit has taken him; he did not make him a child again." It is difficult to know what happens exactly. Some Africans claim that this is a kind of process of civic selection. If the initiation chiefs cannot exact obedience from a given youngster or find that he is unbalanced, vicious or incorrigible and will later bring danger or shame to the clan, they are considered to have rendered a service in getting rid of the young delinquent before he has had a chance to cause trouble for the tribe.

European type schools were opened in West Africa toward the beginning of the nineteenth century and by now they are to be found in all the cities and larger centers. At first, it was difficult to attract pupils. What were the Europeans going to do to the children whom they took for the school? Were they going to take them away to Europe? Would their parents ever see them again? Many an African mother asked herself these questions and many more as her son set off for one of these "new" schools.

In the rural interior, resistance gave way much more slowly. One of my African friends, who in his adult life became a Christian and an important personage in his region, told me how he had begun his schooling.

He was born around 1905 on a beautiful summer night and so was named Youngo. When he was four years old his mother died and two years later he lost his father as well. Youngo belonged to the family of the chief, who entrusted the young orphan to a relative. Set to guarding the latter's flocks, Youngo led a happy carefree life until 1917. That year the French district commissioner asked the chief to send a few boys to the regional school which had been established about twenty miles distant from his village. The commissioner suggested that the chief send his own children, who would thus receive an education and could later be of great help to him.

But at that time in West Africa, no chief was willing to send his own children to school for fear the Europeans would send them to France and they would never come back. Youngo was now eleven or twelve years old. He had no father or mother to defend him and no one to bewail his disappearance. He belonged to the chief's family and so the chief told the commissioner: "This is my son. I will send him to school."

Youngo overheard what was intended for him and fled into the bush, where he lay hidden in the tall grass to escape the misfortune about to befall him. He had heard that the Europeans said they were taking little Africans to school but that in reality they took them to eat them. The chief instituted a search and the hapless Youngo was found and sent to the District Center to school. After a few months, far from enchanted with studying, he ran away again but with no success. The Commissioner asked the chief to send him back and the chief complied.

In the end, Youngo began to enjoy learning and his fears disappeared when months went by and none of his companions were eaten. From primary school he went on for special training and in 1927 became a civil servant. His intelligence and professional integrity quickly won him an enviable reputation and he became a much more important personality than his cousins, the chief's own sons, who had not gone to school.

Still another of my African friends told me that he had not wanted to go to school because he had heard that the Europeans took the pupils' skins to make their shoes. When it became evident that those who went to school attained respectable posts and good salaries, the requests multiplied for more and more schools, at least for the boys. Not so, for the girls, however. Mothers especially were loath to give up the valuable help their bright and clever little daughters gave them in their many long chores.

"Will knowing how to read help her get something to eat?" was a frequent question. "It is much better for her to be a good worker like her mother, better that she knows how to cook, spin, and work the fields."

The advantage of educating girls was more widely accepted when the first midwives, teachers, and civil servants began to contribute part of their salaries to their parents.

Throughout Africa there are still too few schools and the classes are overcrowded, often with sixty or seventy pupils to a room in the primary schools. There is a great difference in the percentage of school attendance between the coastal cities and the villages of the interior. In the former about 40 to 50 per cent of the school age population are enrolled while in the rural areas this drops to about ten or twenty per cent.

Most schools are mission schools. In Nigeria, for instance, Anglican and Catholic missions account for about 70 per cent of the educational effort. In the Cameroun and Ghana, where school enrollment averages about 42 per cent, missions are responsible for the greater part, or 30 per cent of the school age population. In Togo and Dahomey, the number of pupils is about evenly divided between government and mission schools. The situation is understandable when one remembers that the missions were the first to open schools in any of these regions.

Schools for girls, however, are both fewer and smaller than those for boys. One reason advanced for this is the need of the former colonial authorities to train employees for the administration, for commercial purposes and other needs. But African resistance to the education of girls held them back for a long time and still prevents them in many areas from attending the schools that have been opened for them.

Even in the cities where parents are anxious to send their

daughters to school, there is a great lack of classrooms and teachers. Despite the major efforts made over the past ten years, it may be said in general that four out of every five pupils are boys. In Nigeria the proportion is three boys to one girl. The aim is to provide education equally for all — at least through primary school to begin with — and this will come with time.

The first secondary schools were established after World War I in Achimota in Ghana and Ibadan in Nigeria, although some young Africans had already gone on to university studies in England. The minor seminaries of the Catholic missions also provided secondary education for those considering the priesthood. If they did not go on to theological studies and become priests, they had the advantage of good secondary training, and many later achieved positions of distinction.

The principal cities of West Africa — Dakar, Bamako, Conakry, Abidjan, Lagos — soon established secondary schools, and after World War II Achimota and Ibadan were extended to full universities. Three years ago the University of Ghana was transferred to a magnificent new plant and campus at Legon, where a thousand young men and women work for their degrees in highly attractive as well as modern surroundings and in an atmosphere of great intellectual seriousness.

In 1954, the University of Ibadan also moved into handsome modern quarters and now numbers 1200 male students and about 100 women on its rolls. In Zaria in Northern Nigeria there is the College of Arts, Sciences, and Technology, where another thousand students are following courses in engineering, teaching, architecture, agronomy, and commercial sciences.

In the French-speaking countries many families were already sending their sons to French universities at the turn of the century. The number increased appreciably at the end of World War I and since then there have been African students in almost all the French universities.

In 1946, the University of Dakar was founded with the same faculties as French universities. It now numbers about 1500 male students (380 of whom are of French origin) and 200 women students, among whom 70 are African. Some African families still prefer to send their children to France, however, in the belief that they will make faster progress there. Within the past ten years, 15,000 Africans have received their degrees from French universities, while another eight or ten thousand studied in French secondary or technical schools.

The lack of educational facilities in Africa is now a well-known refrain. It is quite true that there are not enough primary schools to accommodate all the children who appear for registration. But there are still other youngsters whose situation is just as serious. These are children who have not attended school before their ninth year and now see the school doors closed to them irrevocably despite their great desire for education. In addition to increasing the number of primary schools, there should also be remedial schools to take care of these children who did not have the opportunity of going to school two or three years sooner. Given their intense will to learn they will soon catch up with their more privileged little peers.

There is a tremendous need for vocational or technical schools on the post-primary and secondary levels, as well as for courses in the psychology of the African child and the pedagogical methods best suited to his development.

In sub-Saharan Africa, parents who have themselves had some education understand that there are lessons and studying to be done at home. But others who have had no such advantage, and particularly relatives who board youngsters whose parents do not live in the school town or city, often require them to perform a number of services and chores that deprive them of time they need for homework.

Then there are those parents who, as in all other countries, think the school should do everything and blame the teacher for any inadequacies in the training of their children. They are a little like the Bambara father who brought his seven-year-old daughter to the mission school and said to the Sister in charge: "I am bringing you my daughter so that she will learn everything she needs to know. Train her well. If she does not obey, you may beat her, but be careful not to tear her dress."

Many Africans feel that since the government schools include no religious training in their curricula, the education they impart lacks a sound moral foundation. Profoundly religious themselves, they wish their children to be God-fearing. Both pagan and Muslim parents often send their children to mission schools even though there is a government school in the vicinity because, they say, "there is no moral or religious training there, but just instruction. And if our children do not believe in God, they will become good-for-nothings."

Juvenile delinquency was formerly very rare in sub-Saharan Africa. Children were strictly reared. The duty to respect and obey their parents and relatives and the clan elders was deeply inculcated in their earliest years. In addition, the average African childhood is a happy time and the African joy of living is a very real thing.

190

Today what juvenile delinquency there is is to be found mainly in the cities and its causes are the universal ones — broken homes, alcoholism, poverty, emotional maladjustment.

There was some alcoholism before the advent of the European in Africa, where the customary local brews of millet, corn, or bananas are often quite heady and intoxicating. There is also strong liquor distilled from palm wine, or corn, banana, pineapple, and other local concoctions. But in former times the African might get drunk only four or five times a year on the occasion of some great customary feast or celebration, or on the occasion of a marriage or funeral. Now there are little liquor shops almost everywhere, selling for the most part very inferior brands, while the cities have their quota of bars and the custom has grown of taking a drink or two every day.

While those who can afford it drink whiskey, gin, or cognac, those who cannot either drink wine or make their own mixtures of European apéritifs and African beer or even mixtures rendered more lethal with eau de cologne or rubbing alcohol.

The result has been an increase in alcoholism against which doctors and missions have raised a cry of alarm, now joined by a number of anti-alcoholism movements among Africans in coastal cities.

Then there are the boys sent to stay with relatives in the city while they attend school but who are more or less neglected by their host families. If they happen to fail in school or are dismissed for bad conduct, they are ashamed to go home to their parents and unwilling to return to work in the fields. Such boys often band together under the leadership of a twelve- or fifteen-year-old and embark on a career of pickpocketing or housebreaking. Whatever they

191

steal — food, clothing, or other objects — is brought back to the leader, who divides the food among them. The rest of the loot they try to sell. Sometimes the sister or little girl friend of one of the boys undertakes to sell the stolen goods in the market. If a boy is caught he never reveals the name of the leader, and more often than not he is released for lack of sufficient evidence against him. To imprison these youngsters merely means putting them with adult thieves who would teach them more than they already know as well as a few other vices.

This problem arose before most of the West African states achieved independence and re-education centers were established by French and British authorities in Senegal, Mali, Ivory Coast, Upper Volta, Niger, Togo, Ghana, Nigeria, and Cameroun. Boys sent to them by the courts are given vocational training and an attempt is made to develop their own creative abilities. There is generally an air of camaraderie among the boys in these centers, where they enjoy also a certain amount of liberty with permission to visit their families on Sundays if they live within a reasonable distance.

In Ghana six such rehabilitation centers have been established for boys in recent years and three for girls, and the program includes placing the children in good foster homes where they may enjoy the benefits of the family life and care previously denied them.

Stealing is not common among girl delinquents. They tend rather to receive and sell stolen goods. In traditional rural areas, it is extremely rare to find a girl who steals. Obviously girls find other ways of earning money which are more lucrative. Here again, the girls involved are most often exploited by the relatives with whom they have been sent to live in the city. The chores imposed on them for their board and keep may be too heavy, while they receive no pocket money and frequently precious little clothing. So they set out to earn money in the only way they can.

The relative in whose care such a girl has been entrusted pays little or no attention to her until she becomes pregnant. Then her arms are raised in horror, her scoldings are many and sharp, and usually she sends the girl home to her parents accusing her of vicious habits.

Occasionally a mother or host relative may actually exploit a girl — more often under the impulse of severe poverty than from motives of gain. The girl will be sent at siesta time to a European ostensibly to sell fruit or some African souvenir. She is told to be charming and gracious and admonished that if the European gentleman takes a fancy to her so much the better.

One of my friends, who had come to Africa to help in the missions, told me that on one occasion a tour with a vaccination unit brought him to a rather remote interior village, where he decided to spend the night. His "boy" was busy preparing supper when a pretty young girl of fifteen or sixteen, wearing an elegant long white cloth that revealed every graceful motion of her lovely body, arrived at his lodging and straightway sat down at his feet.

"Mother told me to spend the night with you," she said simply, "and perhaps you will give me fifty cents."

At that time and in that area fifty cents was enough to feed a family for several days. My friend wondered if the girl, though so elegantly dressed, came perhaps from an impoverished family but that was not the time to inquire.

"Don't you know that God forbids your doing that with someone to whom you are not married?" he asked.

The girl regarded him with wide-eyed incomprehension.

"Who is the God who forbids that?" she asked.

My friend began an explanation that soon became a catechism lesson. The girl, whose name was Sware, listened eagerly and to repay her attention he gave her twenty-five cents and sent her home.

"If you wish to learn more of God's ways," he said as she left, "come back tomorrow."

The following day she returned with her brothers and sisters. After chatting with them a while my friend walked home with them and was astonished to find that the family was fairly well off. After the customary greetings and, noting that the mother accepted his presence cordially, he took occasion to ask her why she had sent him her daughter the evening before.

"Oh," she replied, "that is the first time I have done it. But I have seen many of my neighbors send their daughters to spend the night with a European who was passing through the village and they always came back the next day with money. So I thought, why shouldn't I send my daughter too."

Sware afterward came to the mission school where I met her and we became friends. She later became a Christian, married a fellow Christian, and now has four handsome children.

Such incidents, however, are the exception rather than the rule. As I said earlier, most African mothers watch over their daughters carefully so that they will remain virgins until they are married.

Apart from the other — and more common — causes of juvenile delinquency there is also in Africa that of the breakdown of the old moral framework of customary society, with its attendant fear of customary punishments and the magic objects that indicated the protection of a guardian genie or spirit. For example, a piece of rope twined around a tree trunk, a small bag or sack set conspicuously in a field or against the door of a house gave notice that the owner had been to the diviner, who entrusted the fruits of the tree or the field, or the contents of the house, to a powerful spirit that would severely punish any thief. Fear of this punishment was a strong restraining influence and if anyone had the temerity to steal anyway he paid for it dearly.

Before the period of European domination in West Africa, a thief caught in the act within the compound was killed. If he stole by day in a field, the punishment was several blows of the lash. If he stole by night he was put in chains for several days. In all cases, the thief's family had to pay damages or return the stolen goods. If the thief was a repeater, and especially if he stole at night, he was put to death.

The European administrations abolished these punishments and substituted prison sentences. "This punishment is too light," the African notables used to say. "The thief is lodged and fed, sometimes better than the other members of his family. For when a young man is in jail near his home, his mother prepares all his favorite dishes and brings them to him. He does not have to work hard and so when he comes out he begins all over again."

Recently President Sekou Touré of Guinea restored the death penalty for repeaters. Two young men, twenty and twenty-five years of age respectively, were shot for having committed a theft after being pardoned and released from prison in the general amnesty decree of September 28, 1959. The executions, two months apart, were held in public.

Obviously there are other solutions for the problem where

it exists. African children must have the same opportunities and chance of success as the children of other countries, and for this they must have an education suited to their needs and talents. Up to now, young men with some education all aspired to white collar jobs, but other occupations are necessary for the development of their countries, especially in agriculture and industry.

It is understandable that a young man who has been to school is not enthusiastic about leading the same kind of life as his ancestors in a rural community. But the villages can be modernized, agricultural occupations can be given status through better methods, improved conditions, and better housing. Of special importance in many of the countries are the mass education and community development programs aimed at just such results. Also of great importance is the development of rural welfare services.

Mention should be made of the excellent results achieved by the community development program in Ghana, which will undoubtedly expand as more Africans receive social welfare training.

Most West African cities have social welfare centers, where courses in home economics and child care are greatly appreciated by the women.

Finally, the voluntary investment of good will and human effort will ensure work for the young people and at the same time pride in the endeavors necessary for the progress of their countries.

10. Economic Life

Economic underdevelopment in Africa is usually taken to mean that there is little or no industry, that despite under-nourishment people in general do not have a difficult life, work little and are content with the slow pace of time, which alternates pretty much between dancing and rest. In reality, economic activity in Africa is centuries old, dating from the time when conquering tribes from the East took the territories from the indigenous inhabitants who lived from fishing, hunting, and gathering wild fruits. The new arrivals had other needs and a different standard of living. They developed the countries they conquered, introducing new crops and new crafts. Regular markets for local commerce flourished within the borders of West African states, while a brisk international trade was carried on with North Africa and with countries whose ships touched the coast. The rulers of these states had their customs houses and a system of import and export taxes.

This economy was very similar to that of Europe before the introduction of the steam engine and the development of industry. The latter transformed European and American life, and to a certain extent they have begun to transform African life. Many regions, however, are still untouched and millions of African men and women lead a wholesome and peaceful existence whose work cycle is determined by the changing seasons of the year.

Farming occupies about 60 to 70 per cent of Africa's people. Each family group cultivates what is necessary to feed all its members. The basic food in forest regions is the cassava root and fruit, principally bananas. Their cultivation is the work of women, while men do the heavier work such as clearing the fields of brush and stumps. In the savanna the basic food crop is millet or sorghum. The millet stalks sometimes grow to a height of twelve or thirteen feet and when they ripen often rise above the houses, hiding a whole village from view. Red millet is also grown and used to make beer. Corn, cotton, and peanuts are the other common crops.

The rainy season lasts about four months and is therefore a busy time of digging, sowing, and weeding. The compound chief organizes the work and assigns the different tasks to be done. Ordinarily men and women work the fields together, but in certain tribes the sowing is done by the women only, in the belief that they somehow communicate their own fertility to the earth.

After the eight-month long dry season, the ground is hard as rock and untillable until the first rains fall. Then, the people are out at the earliest moment to prepare their fields for sowing. The wild brush is pulled up and burned on the spot, the ashes serving as fertilizer. This is the time when pagan Africans offer the customary sacrifices to the guardian spirits of the fields and the Christians ask the priest to bless their seeds.

Sowing is a difficult process, and the sower is bent double

throughout. I have often seen women doing it for long hours with their babies slung on their backs. The sower makes a small hole in the earth with a hoe, drops in a few seeds, and covers the hole with a swift movement of the hoe or a bare heel.

When the millet begins to grow, other crops — corn, cotton, rice, green beans, peanuts — are planted. Weeding is incessant and a task at which men and women usually work together. Women must also grow the herbs and other ingredients — such as tomatoes, onions, sorrel, peppers — used in the stew or sauce that always accompanies the millet. Youngsters usually help their mothers with this work, and sometimes they are given a little field of their own or are allowed to gather fruits in the bush and to sell their own small harvests in the market. What they earn they may use as they please.

Men, women, and children do the harvesting together. Generally the men cut down the stalks and the women and children cut off the spikes (which contain the seed) and gather them in baskets. Among certain groups the men thresh the millet; in others the women thresh enough each day for use in preparing the evening meal.

Sometimes a man will invite his friends and all who perhaps owe him some favor to help him the day he digs his fields or harvests his crop. They begin at dawn and work all day to the beat of the drum. In the evening, the host offers a big feast with plenty of meat and millet beer. He then must aid his friends in return. If he is a notable he will send his friends the same number of workers they have loaned him. But work in the chief's fields is part of the tribute each of his subjects owes him — so many days a year to help with the sowing, weeding, and harvesting. On

199

the occasion of local celebrations, everyone partakes of the feast the chief offers to all who come to pay their respects.

During the dry season it is possible to grow vegetables in certain humid areas, but since they were not familiar items in the diet it usually did not occur to Africans to cultivate them. Back in 1935, however, one of my very good African friends, the chief of the province of Koupela in Upper Volta, ordered his subjects to plant fruit trees, to keep them watered from October to June, and to plant kitchen gardens. Today this area furnishes fruits and vegetables to towns within a 300 mile radius, and this constitutes an appreciable source of revenue for the growers.

In the Niger valley, an agency originally created by the French administration — The Niger Office — placed under irrigation about 80,000 acres between Bamako and Timbuktu in Mali. This permitted the establishment of village settlements and the cultivation of rice. The settlers received a house, a plot of ground, oxen, and a light plow free of charge. In the beginning they hesitated to go to the new lands but now about 25,000 settlers are established there and each year hundreds of families await the building of new villages in order to share in the project.

Agronomists and agricultural experts give the general directives for the area but each family chief divides the work to be done among his brothers and sons. After the rich harvest — gathered with modern methods — each family keeps what it needs for the year. The rest of the crop is sold by the co-operative. Each family averages about $1,000 to $2,000 a year from this sale. This is a considerable sum for the growers, who in their native villages grew barely enough to live on and often went hungry when their provision of millet ran out before the next harvest.

Advantage is taken of the dry season to build new houses or repair the old. The wife carries the water to make the mud bricks, while her husband kneads the clay with chopped straw, packs it into wooden frames and lets it dry in the sun. During this season also, any necessary repairs are made to the roofs of the houses, whether thatch or clay. In Mali and Upper Volta the thatch must be repaired every two or three years. The thick roofs of thatch fashioned by the Bamileke in the Cameroun last as long as ten years. At present corrugated iron is being used more and more for roofing.

African governments are doing what they can to increase agricultural production and improve methods. In some areas, like the Niger valley mentioned above, a start has been made toward mechanized farming; in others light plows and tractors have been introduced. Most Africans, however, still use traditional methods because they believe they are best suited to their country. Research centers are experimenting with new crops and training young farmers in new methods, and gradually these will prove their worth. For example, cultivating millet in the traditional way yields about 360 pounds of seed per acre. With the use of a light plow and proper fertilizer this yield is doubled.

Export crops were introduced into West Africa many years ago. The most important of these are peanuts and cotton in the savanna, cocoa and coffee in the forest region. Many plantations of coffee, cocoa, ebony, or palm are owned by Africans.

Here, too, the method of cultivation varies from region to region. In Nigeria and Ghana there are family cocoa farms, while in Dahomey there is a kind of sharecropping system used for the palm plantations. The larger plantations employ

201

hired hands, both men and women, and this is true also of the coffee plantations. Women usually are hired to pick the cocoa and coffee beans.

In addition to contributing her share of work to the family's farming or agricultural activities, the African woman is also responsible for all the household chores. The rooms and the courtyard must be swept out each morning after she has fetched the day's water from the well or standpipe; since these may be three or four miles away, it is no easy matter to carry enough for the day's cooking and cleaning needs. Those who live near a river can do their laundry there, where, spread on the bank, it dries quickly in the strong bleaching rays of the hot sun.

In rural areas, a woman must go almost daily to cut firewood in the bush, while the preparation of the evening meal — a combination of milling and cooking — usually takes long hours, as we have seen. In towns, where bread is available, this is often used for breakfast and the traditional food is taken at the noon or evening meal.

Along the coast there are mechanized mills which free women from the wearisome chores of threshing, pounding, and sifting each day's supply of millet flour. They bring their corn or millet in the morning and come back to fetch their flour in the evening. They must pay for this service but the time they gain is usually spent in some type of remunerative work. These mills are also being introduced in the interior, but many African women cling to the old ways, claiming that the hand milled flour is finer. The other, they claim, is not sifted carefully enough and is not suited to their fancier preparations.

Methods of cooking and seasoning vary from region to

202

region, and Africa has its mediocre cooks as well as excellent *cordon bleus*. Every housewife has her own cherished recipes, which she varies according to the season and the taste of her family. In rural areas, however, a woman's culinary talent is measured by the stew that always accompanies the porridge or rice. Bananas are served broiled or fried, or they may be mashed and served with a sauce. The latter may be a simple mixture of shea butter, pepper and salt, together with a fermented mixture made with *néré* beans. There is also an excellent stew made of mashed peanuts, baobob leaves (or the stalk of the kapok flower), shea butter, sorrel, and vegetables. Onions, tomatoes, green or red peppers, fish (fresh or dried) palm oil (in the forest areas) are other common ingredients. Meat is cooked separately, and the juice then poured into the sauce.

Desserts are few and quite unlike French pastry or Arab cakes. There are fritters or pancakes made of the different types of flour, given to children as a reward. There is also a kind of cookie made of roast peanuts mixed with pepper and honey. In the cities, European foods are coming more and more into use, although practically all families will have the traditional African food for at least one meal.

In traditional areas, the African drinks water with his meals. The native beer is reserved for special occasions and the customary feasts or celebrations. Although breweries, too, exist in the larger centers, in rural areas it is the housewife who makes the beer.

I have often watched Ambwo, an African housewife, make millet beer, which she does about once a week, and which for her is a profitable undertaking. She has an agreement with a relative to keep her regularly supplied with red millet. She lets it sprout and then dries it. She next hires a few women to pound it between two stones. Meanwhile, she fills with water a row of tall jars, each containing about six gallons, set against the wall of her courtyard. The pounded millet is poured into the jars, under each of which a small fire is lighted. For two days she keeps these fires going, watches over the simmering mixture, skimming it from time to time. On the third day she adds the leaven and keeps the liquid simmering for another whole day. Then, according to ancient custom, she adds liana twigs, the bark of which produces fermentation and the mixture is allowed to cool overnight. In the morning the beer is fizzing and bubbling and is ready to be drunk. Ambwo does not put liana twigs in two of the jars, however, because some of her customers prefer unfermented beer. Sometimes this is ordered especially to celebrate the birth of a child.

In the savanna, shea butter is the fat most used for cooking, while in forest areas it is palm oil. And it is the women who must make these products also.

The fruit of the small shea-butter trees resembles a skimpy green plum. Its white sweetish meat surrounds a large nut, the kernel of which is its chief value. When my friend Simbazere sent us shea-butter fruit with her daughter Cecile, we at the mission school always carefully kept the nuts, because we knew Cecile would come for them a few days later.

Making shea butter is not a simple process. The nuts are kept under water for several weeks. After they are dried in the sun they are roasted in a special homemade oven. After this, the kernels, which resemble nutmegs are removed and put back in the oven to dry thoroughly. Then the kernels are pounded in a mortar kept just for this purpose, because the process yields a fatty, chestnut-colored paste with a strong, lingering odor. This paste is ground further between the millstones, and produces a thick semiliquid, that looks a little like chocolate pudding. It is now poured into a large jar and worked with both hands while warm and cold water is poured in alternately in order to separate the fat from the residue. Energetic kneading causes the paste to whiten and foam, and after about an hour and a half of this, the butter rises to the top, is gathered into other pots, and boiled over a hot fire for several hours. As this cools, the sediment goes to the bottom of the jar and the fat rises to the surface. Before it is entirely cool, however, it is decanted into other pots. The residue, a mixture of fat and sediment, is strained separately. Within a couple of days, the shea butter solidifies and looks like margarine.

This shea butter is sold in the market or kept for a variety of home uses, such as making soap and as a salve or beauty cream. Set in a shallow bowl with a rag for a wick it also serves as fuel for illumination. Now in the markets there are iron lamps hung from stands that are easily set in an earthen floor, very much like the iron lamps attached to a hook and hung from the wall in the farms of southern Europe not too long ago.

To make soap, lye, which is made from wood ashes in the traditional manner, is boiled with shea butter and stirred constantly until it forms a soft gray ball. When it cools it is cut into cakes of different sizes and left to dry. In two days it is ready for market.

Thousands of tons of shea butter also find their way to Europe each year, to be used in making chocolate candy, soap, and stearic acid.

In the forest regions, palm oil takes the place of shea butter. When the palm fruit is ripe, men climb up the tall trees and cut it down with large knives. After the nuts are removed the fruit is put into a large earthen pot, covered with water and boiled over a hot fire for two hours while it is being constantly stirred with a huge wooden paddle. This mixture is allowed to cool and is then poured off into smaller jars, which are carried to the bank of a nearby stream. Here in a kind of vat of stones surrounded by a low wall, the fruit, which has swelled in the cooking, is trodden on and thus reduced to a thick paste. When water is poured over this, the oil rises to the surface. This oil is skimmed off and set to boil, again in earthen pots. During the hours of boiling, the foam is skimmed from the oil, which begins to lighten to a reddish orange color. When the oil cools it is poured into tall bottles or aluminum cans. This, too, has a variety of household uses besides serving as a cooking fat.

Still another oil is derived from the nut of the fruit, but this is exported. When the women finish making their own oil, they gather the palm nuts, crush them and extract the kernels, which they sell in the market or take to the factory where this type of oil is pressed out by machine. The factories either buy directly from the producers or, in certain areas, send trucks through the village marketplaces to buy up the palm kernels.

Soap is also made from palm oil, in much the same way as shea-butter soap. It takes about two weeks to dry out and be ready for market. Manufactured soap is available now in African markets and the women often buy this for personal use, reserving the homemade soap for laundry since it has a very strong bleaching action.

Formerly all utensils in West Africa were earthenware of local make. Now enamel basins and iron pots of all sizes are purchasable in most marketplaces and these have the prized advantage of being unbreakable.

But African women who make pottery, which they sell more cheaply than the imported utensils, still find a fairly large market for their wares. Some prefer the earthen pots out of loyalty to traditional methods, others claim that some foods taste better when they are cooked slowly in the old way in earthen pots. In some regions, like Northern Ghana, all the women make pottery, but in others it is the special industry of experts who never reveal the secrets of their trade, even though they work in their open courtyard where everyone can see them.

One of my Yoruba friends, Titilayo, makes especially good pottery. Her name means "joy forever" because she brought joy to her family by her birth. Everyone calls her "Titi" for short, and with her smiling happy nature she lives up to her name.

"Can you use any type of earth for the pots?" I asked her.

"No; it must be earth that will harden well. And then you have to sift it carefully to make sure there are not little stones or other impurities left in it."

When the earth is not the best quality, it is mixed with the dust of old pots that have been finely crushed between two stones.

Titilayo does not have a potter's wheel and so it takes her several days to fashion one pot. She uses the bottom of an old one on which to fashion the new, spreading over it layers of new clay, welding them carefully and smoothing them with a flat wet stone. When the pot or vase is a certain size, she lets it dry for a day or two, and then begins to build it up again layer by layer. Sometimes she lets the finished pot dry for a while before adding the handles, or in the case of a vase, the neck. She then polishes it glass smooth with a stone or a small wet board. Designs are etched on the pot with a stone wound with thread, or with a piece of metal, or by pressing against it a copper bracelet that is ornamented with designs.

The pot must then dry for several days before it is ready to be baked. Titilayo generally waits until she has several ready, when she and her friends work together to fire them. For firing, the pots are piled one on the other, with twigs or millet stalks between and inside them, and then the piles are covered with small sticks of wood which are set afire. For about five hours, Titi and her friends keep the fire going at high heat, which bakes the pots a dark red. By the next day they are cool and the women have no difficulty recognizing their own pots by the different designs. Many, however, crack or burst in the process, and these are ground to powder and used in the next batch. Those that are not baked enough are porous and will be set aside for the next firing. If two thirds of the pots emerge successfully it has been a good day.

Weaving of mats and other basketwork is done by both men and women, depending on the tribe. In some, the women do the mats, the men the large baskets. Materials are stalks of grass, palm leaves, raffia or sisal fibers, according to region. These are dried first in the sun and then soaked in water for several hours to make them pliable. A strip of bark is often used to bind a mat or basket so that it will keep its shape. Strips of leather are also used to finish baskets and to bind the rims of the big woven hats worn by the Mossi of Upper Volta and the Dagomba of Ghana, which are adorned besides with pieces of leather artistically shaped.

In some tribes of Upper Volta and Northern Ghana, a pregnant woman weaves a flat rectangular basket about twenty-four inches long to serve as the baby's cradle. The Dagari add a cover to protect the baby from the sun when they carry baby, basket, and all on their heads. A Lobi mother carries the basket suspended from a leather cord around her neck. The Bobo-Fing, who carry their babies on their back, use the cradle only to put the child to sleep at home. If the baby dies, the cradle is destroyed.

Women and girls also weave straw or grass into belts, bracelets, necklaces, and headpieces, frequently with highly complicated and delicate designs. Woven straw or cane is sometimes used to make the pads on which they carry objects of varying shape and size and up to a weight of eighteen or twenty pounds perfectly balanced on their heads. More often these pads are made of rolled cloth.

Cotton has been cultivated for centuries in the savanna. Men and women often have their own separate fields to cultivate, but after the harvest it is the women's task to pick it from the pods and spin it, while weaving is reserved almost everywhere to the men.

Women work at the cotton at odd moments in between their other chores. A tuft of raw cotton is placed on a flat stone and then rolled around a small piece of metal or wood. This detaches the seeds, which are kept apart. The seeds, which have an astringent property, are crushed and added to the evening stew.

The carding is done with a simple instrument, two combs made of boards and nails. The spindle is a small wooden rod with a terra cotta ball at the bottom. The distaff with its hunk of raw cotton is held steady in the left hand. A little is pulled out and wound around the spindle, which is then twirled like a top. When the spindle is full, the cotton thread is wound into balls, and when there are enough of these to make a garment the housewife takes them to the weaver.

I remember a certain Nab'Youre who is still the best weaver in his village. His cloths are tightly woven, and he accepts only the smoothest spun cotton. His fee is not money but double the cotton necessary for the garment ordered. If he does not have time to weave the extra cloth himself, he has his son do it, and this second garment is sold in the market. This tightly woven cloth is generally used for trousers, while a looser weave is chosen for blouses or shirts. The weavers — many of whom become known for their designs — use a simple hand loom that produces strips of cloth about four inches wide, which are sewn together for the desired garment.

Although some textile factories have been established and ready-made clothes are now available, the products of the local weavers are valued highly. Africans may wear European dress to work, but they will usually wear the traditional costume for feast days or great ceremonies, or for evening wear.

The cloths of certain regions have become famous. Among the best known are the coverlets of Macina, the cloths of Timbuktu, and the Kente cloths of Ghana. A Kente cloth may cost upward of $90 or $100.

In Mali or Upper Volta, a good weaver can finish a cloth in a day if he weaves until sunset with only enough time out at noon for a quick meal. If he lives in a small village, he will ask the equivalent of a dollar for this labor. In Mali I knew a weaver who made the lovely coverlets of Macina. It took him three days to finish one and his price ranged from four to six dollars.

In former times, sewing was also considered to be man's work, and when attempt was made to teach it to girls they invariably replied, "Teach it to the boys, that is man's work." But with the development of home economics courses both in the schools and in social welfare centers, this has changed. In the French-speaking countries, there are a number of women who have studied in the larger couturier establishments in France. In rural areas, however, tailoring and dressmaking is still man's province.

Trading and commerce have always been brisk in West Africa. In the Middle Ages camel caravans crossed the Sahara from North Africa bringing to the banks of the Senegal and Niger their cargoes of textiles, copper, jewelry, guns, and gunpowder, and especially those bars of rock salt that are still to be found in the markets of the interior. The arrival of the caravans was the occasion of public celebrations, which are recorded in history. The West African markets provided the North with gold dust, ivory, kola nuts, and slaves to be sold to the chiefs and notables of the Sahara, Algeria, Tunisia, and Morocco.

There was also a busy trade by sea, which enriched the royal treasuries of the time through customs duties and taxes. But besides this type of commerce, there was and still is, the trading in the local markets in which women play a very important role.

It is to the local village market, settled informally in the shade of a tree or at a crossroads, that African women bring their shea butter or beer, their pottery or soap. Beer and food vendors will always be found near the place where a marriage or funeral of a notable is taking place, or any other event that draws large numbers of people. There are other famous markets in the large urban centers, said to be

300 or 400 years old, to which traders come a three days' journey on foot to buy or sell their products. These markets grew up either along an important route or near a navigable river — "wherever one may go on foot or by boat" according to an African saying.

If a chief wished to set up a market in his area, either to increase its influence or to introduce new products, he would first consult the elders of the village. If they were agreed, he next went to the diviner to make sure the proposed market would not bring any misfortune or trouble upon the village. If the omens were favorable, then a bull or red roosters were offered in sacrifice. Their blood was poured on stones set at the two extremities of the place chosen for the market. Then the market day was decided upon. Often this was the anniversary day of the founding of the village. If this was unknown — which was rarely the case — some day of augury was chosen, like Monday, which brings glory, or another day held to be a bringer of good fortune in the local tradition.

This explains why some fairly large villages lack markets. Either the omens were unfavorable or the elders were afraid the establishment of a market would invite raids from a pillaging tribe.

Markets are held, then, on different days in different villages, and I have known women in Mali who, before the advent of trucks, went each day to one or another in a neighboring village, sometimes covering on foot a distance of eight or ten miles each way. In any case, it is easy to know which day is market day in any African locality, for one sees long lines of people, and especially women, coming and going, carrying on their heads the merchandise they are going to sell or the products they have bought.

In the savanna, one finds both men and women traders in the markets. Usually they live in the vicinity and are selling the products of their own farm or crafts.

Women are generally to be found selling foodstuffs — rice, millet, green beans, oil, fresh milk, or curds. These are sold by weight, and the measure may vary slightly from one vendor to the next. Peanuts, tomatoes, and other ingredients for the perennial sauce are arranged in little piles and sold by the pile. Fruit is generally sold by the piece.

Matches, candles, bleaching soap, safety pins, nails, locks are other items sold by women. Others cook tasty fritters in palm oil, whose sizzling fragrance attracts traders and clients alike.

Beside a butcher's display of raw meat, a young apprentice may be broiling chunks of meat on a spit over a wood fire. Men generally come to market to sell goats, burros, skins, basketwork, or strips of hand woven cloth, tools such as hoes and pickaxes, and beads of all kinds and sizes.

Traders who go from one market to another — the traveling salesmen of Africa — generally handle European textiles, shoes, sandals of local make, coverlets, clothing, wooden bowls, enamel basins, and iron pots, and a wide variety of leather goods — from purses to saddles.

The most important products of all those sold in the markets of the savanna, however, are salt and kola nuts and a number of sayings attest to this. For example, a popular person is described as being "beloved as a kola merchant," since the latter is often surrounded by a circle of admirers. When a favor is sought and the answer is long in coming, a common plea is, "Please, put salt in my stew" — that is, please give me a favorable reply. An African who is furious

213

with an enemy will exclaim by way of a curse, "May God put no salt in him."

In former times, all the salt sold in the region came from the salt mines of Taoudenit in the Sahara. Now, however, European salt is also to be found in the markets and shops. Since during the rainy season it tends to become soggy it has not yet dethroned the rock salt, still widely used especially in the villages of the interior.

Because of its effect as a stimulant, kola also has a social function. Among most of the tribes of Senegal, Mali, Upper Volta, and Niger, there is no matrimonial contract or friendy alliance made without a gift of kola nuts. They are presented to a chief or an older person as a sign of respect and are also a proper gift of thanks for a service rendered. A present of kola nuts to a woman or young girl is a token of affection and even of love. In other words, the African says it with kola nuts instead of with flowers.

Salt and kola merchants, therefore, enjoy special consideration. They often frequent only the markets near their place of residence, but they also make the rounds of the markets of a region, carrying their merchandise on their heads or traveling by truck when they can.

Finally, every market in the savanna has its little water vendors — eight or nine year old girls who for a penny, a pinch of salt, or a fruit will provide a calabash of water for a thirsty buyer or for a mammy trader who cannot leave her wares.

In the Benin gulf area, from Ghana to Nigeria, almost all trading seems to be in the hands of women. Many have a highly varied inventory — rice, corncakes, condiments, cassava, cigarettes, mirrors, bluing, candles, matches, soap — which brings them a profit of from ten to twenty dollars a month. The more prosperous traders handle cloths and such objects as belts, sunglasses, perfumes, and costume jewelry, Ovaltine, canned goods, which may net them from thirty to sixty dollars a month.

There are also a few very rich traders, who sell luxury items and elegant clothing and cloths. One such woman trader in Ghana was reported recently as selling between fifty and sixty cloths per day at ten or twelve dollars each, thereby grossing about $150,000 to $200,000 per year. Her monthly profit was said to be between $1,000 and $1,500. In Nigeria, I was told of a trader from Ibadan whose gross averaged $10,000 a month, with a net profit of about $1,000. These, however, are exceptions, for the most prosperous generally average a net profit of about $300 per month.

Some African women own trucks, a fact which permits them to have partners in other towns, but trade between countries does not depend on private means of transportation. Women traders from Dahomey, for instance, will go to markets in Nigeria by public conveyance dressed in an old cloth. On the way home, they will be wearing several new cloths over new undergarments, which they will sell the next marketday.

There is brisk trading between Dahomey, Togo, and Ghana, as well as between Ghana and Upper Volta. In Dahomey, Nigeria, and Togo, women make beauty creams or perfumes, jealously guarding their recipes. They send their young servant girls to sell these from house to house along with combs, imported perfume, ribbons, and a whole array of other novelties.

African women have a very keen sense of business, inherited perhaps from their ancestors who were organized in guilds over 150 years ago. The market women of

215

Abeokuta in Nigeria went on a famous strike during the past century to protest an increase in taxes. Since they held the monopoly of trade their strike seriously upset the economy of the whole region. Food supplies dwindled, the unhappy public took sides with the numerous market women who were their relatives or friends, and the king had to give in and lower the rates.

Organizations of market women still exist both along the coast and in the interior. In the towns of Mali and the Upper Volta, women who have recently undertaken the brewing of beer and do not yet have a steady clientele, prefer to form groups of eight or ten to divide the work and then share the profits.

A woman who sells the soap or shea butter she has made herself needs no capital to set up shop in the market. Those who must buy their wares need quite a bit or at least good credit. Sometimes a woman is given her start in business by her mother but more often she acquires her capital in other ways.

In certain tribes of Dahomey and Togo, a husband who finds his bride is a virgin will on the morning after the wedding night, give her a gift of money according to his own means — and this may vary from five to fifty dollars. With this the bride can start a business of her own choosing.

Where this custom does not obtain, a woman who wishes to start trading must seek credit. This is easy enough in her own town where she is known to be honest and a hard worker. But if her marriage takes her to another town, she must find someone who will introduce her to a supplier and guarantee the payment for the merchandise he gives her on credit. Her first such acquisition may be about $15 worth of varied wares, and after that the amount of credit given her increases. If for several years she has made good on every transaction, she may receive as much as $100 credit, especially at Christmas and Easter time and during the period of the major local celebrations.

In the Mali region, traders who are well known can obtain loans from rich creditors, but a loan made against a pledge is more common. The pledge is usually some object of value such as gold or silver jewelry, a rich cloth, an animal, a house. In former times, a person could be offered as pledge or security, who then worked for the creditor without salary and without having her work count to reduce the debt. On the other hand, the loan was paid back without interest.

Most market women take to trading from necessity, to earn food for themselves and their children. This is because the husband frequently considers that his salary is his personal property and he keeps it for himself as he would have kept anything he earned, according to traditional custom. If he is more attuned to modern times and the needs of his family and uses all or part of his salary for their support, the wife will continue to trade to raise their standard of living or simply because she likes to go out and see a bit of what's going on in the world. For the market is the great meeting place of different peoples from all points of the compass, and all kinds of news, fruitful contacts, and useful information are to be had there.

Sometimes the mammy trader you meet today began going to market with her mother at the age of six or seven. After thirty or forty years of that variegated bustle she would find it unbearable to stay home and tend only to the housekeeping. That is why she is off to the market with her wares in early morning. If she has cloth to sell she sets up her stall in a covered booth and pays a high license fee. If she sells food products, she spreads her straw mat on the ground and her fee is much less. She sits on the small wooden stool she has brought with her and shades herself from the hot sun with a rush umbrella on a bamboo pole, which she moves as the sun moves. Around her are other traders who are friends rather than competitors. When one has to leave her place, her neighbor sells for her.

A motley swarming crowd mills through the market. Women with babies on their backs and baskets on their heads move from one stall to the other bargaining, weighing a cassava or watermelon in the hand, feeling a cloth, amid a constant exchange of greetings, banter and laughter, and the many-voiced chorus of vendors calling out the merits of their wares and inviting one and all to the privilege of great bargains.

There are the curious who idle slowly around, and travelers charged with a purchase for a friend or relative back home anxiously searching for it through the market. Or a woman from a distant village comes looking for a friend of her sister-in-law so that she may give and get the latest news for both.

Then there are the wary buyers who act as if they were not really interested in making a purchase, and bargain endlessly until the trader either gives in or sends them packing with a sharp word. In the latter case they may come back and say: "I have thought it over; you have good stuff. I'll take it at your last price!"

The unscrupulous may try to take advantage of an inexperienced trader or count on their own charms to buy on credit with no intention of paying. But the market women are usually sharp enough to get rid of any such nuisance with an apt proverb or a quip that arouses general laughter.

I remember the case of one would-be chiseler who made the rounds of a market in Nigeria explaining to each mammy trader that he had left his money home but that he would return the next morning to pay for the handsome cloth he wished to give his wife when their baby was born. He had met with no success when he finally approached my friend Teresa — a veteran of that particular market — who had been watching his progress and had no desire to waste time on him.

"What are you doing here while your wife is suffering?" she asked.

"My wife is suffering?" he repeated, startled by this question from a woman whom he did not know.

"Of course. She is at the maternity clinic about to deliver!"

The man went off on a run, took the first bus to his own village and rushed to the clinic. His wife was not there. Home he dashed to find her calmly going about her chores as usual.

"What happened?" he demanded.

"Nothing has happened," she said, "but I did not expect you until tomorrow so I have not prepared any meal for tonight."

Thirty miles away, Teresa had had a pleased chuckle with her friends.

Sometimes, a trader will get sleepy in the hot sunny air, and to wake herself up will go about the market. She may find a bargain or two, or she may buy some treat for the children who will be out of school when she gets home.

Actually, the market women lead a hard and tiring life, although many of them do not realize the toll it takes. I have often seen them come home almost exhausted. And when they have to wait a while for a bus or train, it is not uncommon to see them stretch out on the ground to rest. They often have to walk a long distance from train or bus to get to the market in the first place, carrying the heavy burden of their wares on their heads. In some towns the busiest time is the evening, and this means very late hours for the traders.

I remember a drive to Lagos one night after a flat tire had delayed us for some time. Although it was ten-thirty at night there was one little stall after another set up all along the way, lit by pressure lamps or lanterns, and the traders, both men and women, seemed as numerous as the clients, so many in fact, that I kept thinking every minute that we were about to enter the city. Actually we were still twenty-five miles from the outskirts. Business became brisker as we approached the capital, and when electric lights suddenly replaced the pressure lamps, we knew we had reached the city limits.

However, in Senegal, Mali, and Upper Volta, some women are not permitted to go to market, either to buy or just to see. They belong to the aristocratic Muslim families who maintain their ancient traditions. Women cannot go out unaccompanied and, for their personal shopping, go to the stores in the city. Shopping for food is done by servants. They are not idle women, however, for they take care of their own lodgings and their children and do some of the cooking with the servants, and all have their share of cotton to comb and spin, and other regular duties.

Every large city now has at least one big department store, where many African girls find work as salesgirls and secretaries. Most of them prefer this type of job to a stall in the market, but it seems the markets will last a long time yet even in the cities that have the large stores. Besides the latter — which were established mostly after World War II — there are the firms of the international commercial houses, the local administration of which is conducted by Africans, who work on commission.

An increasing number of Africans now own their own shops and share the benefits and headaches of small shopkeepers the world over. While this is a recent development, private ownership of a dressmaking or tailoring establishment has been common for a long time. The dressmaking houses have a number of faithful clients and train apprentices, who get a certificate after a course of from three to five years and have no difficulty in developing a following of their own, especially if their prices at the start are somewhat lower than those of the training establishment.

While most means of transportation — i.e., regular train or bus services — are run either by the government or large companies, Africans who own their own trucks or buses do an active business transporting both people and merchandise.

In some regions of Mali and the Upper Volta there are gold mines, once very famous, that have remained family enterprises, but the deposits of which are now not rich enough to warrant modern installations. The owners allow individuals or family groups to work them in return for a percentage of the yield from time to time. The mines are vast places with a number of circular shafts about 25 to 30 inches in diameter and 30 to 40 feet deep. The workers descend by placing their hands and feet in little holes dug in the walls of the shaft. At the bottom, they dig with a small pick and load the pay dirt into a calabash, which is pulled to the top by a rope and lowered the same way. The dirt is sifted and washed several times until only the gold nuggets are left in the bottom of the calabash. There is no ventilation in these mine wells, and the miners can stay down only for a short period of time. They come out exhausted, and I have seen them actually helped to the surface by their fellow workers. After a short rest period they go down again.

Sometimes two or three brothers and their wives and children (ten to fourteen years of age) work together. The youngsters carry the pay dirt to the river, where the women pan it. Unfortunately, these workers are exploited by traders who charge them very high prices even for the foods in season. Thus their hard labor often yields them no more than $200 or $300 for a whole family after seven months of work, since they cannot dig for the gold during the rainy season.

Modern industries are being developed in sub-Saharan Africa — textile mills, rope (from sisal) factories, canneries (fish and fruit), oil-works, soap factories, etc. All of these small industries employ both men and women, and trade unionism is growing.

Finally, Africans are to be found in most other social or professional occupations — civil servants, teachers, doctors, nurses, midwives, social workers, judges, lawyers, sheriffs, notaries, engineers, agronomists — forming the indispensable structure for the well-being and the intellectual, technical, and social progress of the country.

11. Women of the New Africa

During a recent trip through West Africa, I visited the mother of Sister Marie-Jeanne, whom I had known as a young nun of deep spirituality. She had won the admiration of all her colleagues, for though she was the daughter of a great chief she always took on herself the most difficult or irksome tasks. She had died young leaving behind the memory of her example. But I had been only slightly acquainted with her mother, Mathilda, now a widow, living at some distance from the Mission. When I saw her again, poorly dressed, stooped and wrinkled, I was filled with a great feeling of respect: "I am in the presence of the mother of a saint," I thought. And I wondered how, coming from a pagan background, she had been able to give her daughter a training that prepared her for the religious life and the practice of the highest virtue.

But Africa has always had its remarkable women, rich in natural virtue and human worth, who have trained their children to live an honest upright life within the framework of their own custom.

Now the swift changes taking place throughout the continent are forcing new duties upon the women. It is no longer enough for them to increase the number and the

223

prosperity of the clan through their children. They have their special contribution to make in the building of the new Africa. New responsibilities — social, civic, and political — demand their attention, which they can neither escape nor neglect without loss to their country and themselves.

Mme. Quezzin Coulibaly, Minister for Social Affairs of Upper Volta and one of Africa's foremost women leaders, undoubtedly had this in mind when she urged that the many painful features of women's dependent status be eliminated so that they might help to shape the new African civilization. The wave of materialist and utilitarian technology accompanying the evolution of Africa, she said, must not be allowed to drown the African's joy of living and his human and spiritual values. If he is uprooted and cut off from what has been the rationale of his life, he will lose the best part of himself.

Mme. Quezzin Coulibaly, who is the widow of the former Prime Minister of the Upper Volta, is also a member of her country's legislature. Her daughter Denise is one of the first African women to earn a pilot's license.

In the Cameroun another woman leader, Mme. Julienne Keutcha from the Bamileke region, was elected to the National Assembly in April, 1960. Nigeria boasts a woman senator, Mrs. Esan, and women are taking part increasingly in the legislative bodies of the newly independent states. In all West Africa women have been elected to municipal councils and are active in community affairs, to which they bring a different viewpoint from that of their male colleagues and a more sensitive understanding of family needs. Throughout West Africa women have the right to vote and are eligible for election to public office.

In certain regions with a Muslim majority — i.e., Northern Nigeria, the Niger Republic, and certain sections of Mali — custom and public opinion still keep many women from exercising their political rights. Elsewhere the number of women taking an interest in politics is very large, especially in the cities, and they are active in electoral campaigns.

African women are also entering the professions in greater number. They are to be found practicing law, medicine, and dentistry, and there are a few women judges. Nursing, midwifery, social welfare, and teaching, however, claim the greatest number. Most of them work with a spirit of contributing to the future of their country and of helping improve women's status generally.

Women's groups and associations are also becoming increasingly active as well as more numerous. One of my Camerounian friends wrote me recently describing a new organization which she has founded. "Our aim," she writes, "can be summed up in this way: protection of women and young girls; education for women and girls; improving the status of the Camerounian women. We are making a careful study of all the problems affecting women, and we are trying to work out a rural and an urban program that will be suited to their needs. Our aim is both a long range educational program and some concrete action to begin immediately. We are encouraged by the Ministers of Government and all the people, who promise us moral and material help."

Another friend, a civil servant in Dahomey and president of another women's organization, spends every weekend at the maternal and child health clinic run by her group. There are associations to help young working girls and widows to find suitable lodgings in the cities. Still others conduct lit-

225

eracy programs, and gather in women to persuade them of the usefulness of certain government measures, such as vaccination, or to explain the disadvantages of certain old customs, particularly those relating to marriage. These groups also assist young women to obtain their freedom from one or another of these customs either through the courts or through a process of persuasion and reconciliation with whoever exercises over them the rights of family head.

For example, Clotilde, a little Camerounian girl, twelve years old was promised in marriage by her father, who had begun to receive installments on her bride price. Three years later, she fell in love with a classmate and resolved to free herself of the bond her father had contracted for her. With the help of one of the women's groups mentioned above, she took a job as a salesgirl in one of the larger shops and at the end of a year she had saved enough to refund the bride price already paid and to break her engagement. Happy to be free, she is now saving up enough to set up housekeeping, for she and the young man of her choice plan to be married within a year.

These organizations also study the most urgent needs in their respective regions. What priority should be given to the building of new schools, clinics, social welfare centers or adult education centers? The answer differs from one place to the next but in any case pressure is brought to bear on the public authorities.

There are other fields in which women are taking direct action, individually and in organizations, to modify the customary law or to introduce some innovation. In some villages, they conduct campaigns to persuade mothers to send their little girls to school. In others, they convince the more influential families to reduce, by way of example, the exaggerated expenditures that often accompany weddings and funerals and that leave an average family — or young couple — in debt for years. In some cities women's organizations have demanded that film review boards include mothers as members, for they are opposed to films that portray thieving or violence.

Examples might be multiplied but to cite just one, there is the method used by Catholic Action movements summed up in the phrase, "See, judge, act." Applied to daily problems, this encourages in the members a spirit of observation, reflection, and finally action in the interests of the common welfare.

The influence of strong feminine personalities in areas where custom still prevails should not be overlooked, although they may have less education than those we generally think of as leaders. They have the same basic qualities of good sense, courtesy, optimistic good nature, and generosity as their more educated sisters, and they can do much to help their unlettered neighbors and friends to improve, spiritually and materially, their family status.

Among the women deeply concerned with the social progress of their people, special mention must be made of the African Sisters, who in a real sense have pioneered in asserting woman's right to a free choice of her state in life. They have chosen to dedicate themselves to the service of God and of the poor and to work for the development of their country, helping to raise the intellectual, moral, and spiritual level of their fellow men. Sometimes they are working with European Sisters, but increasingly they are developing their own institutions and activities under the direction of their own African Superiors. They are to be found teaching, nursing, doing home visiting, caring for lepers

227

and organizing mass education programs, often despite very limited means.

The latter programs — under the sponsorship of the government social welfare department or of the missions and sometimes aided by UNESCO — are very popular in all West Africa. Courses consist of reading, writing, and simple arithmetic. For the men, there is instruction in improved farming methods, the use of fertilizers, and elementary carpentry. The women have classes in homemaking, child care, and hygiene. In Ghana some 25,000 to 30,000 women attend the mass education courses each year, organized by the government social welfare department.

The status of women in West Africa is very similar to that of women in other areas of the continent. Throughout Africa women are awakening to their own personalities and dignity as women, and women's associations are as many and active in East Africa as in the Western areas. They feel that their status and role in the family conditions their role and activity in the community. Consequently their organizations concentrate mostly on questions affecting the family, marriage customs, education of the children. Their aim is the eventual abolition of those outmoded customs which fetter a woman's freedom or hinder her in the full normal development of her own personality.

Since local associations are often affiliated to a larger group or an international organization, their studies and inquiries concentrate on specific points, and surveys based on replies from several different regions provide valuable information on the persistence of old customs or the progress made in modifying them. Attendance at international congresses affords African women an excellent opportunity to discuss their problems, exchange information on their achievements, outline their hopes and aspirations and engage the interest and support of women throughout the world.

In October, 1957, several African women took part in the international congress of the World Union of Catholic Women's Organizations held in Rome. One workshop was devoted exclusively to African questions, and representatives from eleven African countries discussed the status of women in their respective areas. They insisted upon recognition of their equality with men as human persons, their equal dignity and their equal fundamental human rights, enjoyed by women in many other countries. Their demands were, in fact, modest and recognized for that matter in the Universal Declaration of Human Rights adopted by the United Nations — namely, equal rights for men and women before, during, and after marriage. They requested legal recognition of woman's right to the custody of her children in case of her husband's death or of separation of husband and wife; protection for monogamous marriage and the gradual suppression of polygamy; the abolition of the bride price or at least its limitation to a minimal, symbolic value; courses in preparation for marriage for young men as well as for young women; access to education at all levels and a sound practical training so that they "may take their proper place in the Christian, social, and political development of their country."

In 1958 three women's congresses were held in West Africa to study women's problems. The first took place at Ibadan, Nigeria, in January, and was organized by the World Council of Churches. Thirty women participated, fourteen of whom were Africans from Uganda, Tanganyika, Kenya, Northern Rhodesia, South Africa, Congo, Cameroun, Togo, Nigeria, Sierra Leone, and Liberia.

The second, also organized by the Protestant churches and aimed especially toward the service of women in the Church, was held at Nkongsamba (Cameroun) in February of 1958. This was attended by over a hundred Camerounian women, several ministers and some European missionaries (Protestant).

The third was organized by the World Union of Catholic Women's Organizations in Lome Togo in July of 1958 under UNESCO sponsorship. Three hundred African women from ten countries — Guinea, Ivory Coast, Ghana, Upper Volta, Togo, Dahomey, Nigeria, Cameroun, the two Congos — studied various aspects of woman's life and activities in this transitional period of Africa's history. They were joined by several Protestant Togolese women in a series of workshop discussions all chaired by African women.

Their conclusions were termed a "charter of the rights of the African woman." They declared, among other things, that "woman is equal to man by nature," although this equality is accompanied by different functions, and concluded that woman must be "as free as man to fulfill her personal destiny and to choose her state of life. If she wishes to marry, she should be able to choose her husband freely."

Still another international meeting was held in Bamako, Mali, in July of 1959, organized by the Union of Women of West Africa. It was attended by about a thousand women, most of them Muslim or animist and the rest Christian. They came from Mali, Senegal, Guinea, Upper Volta, and Dahomey.

The conclusions and recommendations adopted by the women in these various congresses are strikingly similar. All opposed child marriage, child betrothal, and polygamy. They urged either that the bride price be entirely abolished or again that it have only a symbolic and quite neglible monetary value. They all asserted the right of widows to the custody of their children and condemned the custom of inheriting widows. They asked that the free consent of the spouses be made an obligatory condition for marriage and they favored the setting of a minimum age for marriage as well as the compulsory registration of marriages. The Catholic and the Protestant seminars urged *inter alia* legal protection for monogamous marriage, establishment of the legal right of monogamous couples to acquire joint property and the right of their children to inherit this directly, the abolition of female circumcision, and marriage preparation courses for both young men and young women.

This unanimity among African women of different countries and different social backgrounds proves that they all have the same ideal of the family even if their religion permits polygamy. The same unanimity appears again in their desire for the development of education for girls and for the participation of women in the civic and political life of their countries.

To avoid repetition, I quote only from the conclusions of the Lome congress, which are the more detailed on this subject: "Those participating in this study session affirm the necessity to intensify the preparation of the African girl for the increasing responsibilities which await her in the Africa of today.

"Considering that, compared to boys, girls too often receive unfavorable treatment both at home and in their studies, the seminar participants ask that many girls' schools be opened — primary, secondary, and technical. In these schools, the Africanized curriculum should be adapted to the psychology of the young girl and to her role in African society. Adequate domestic science teaching, preparing the woman for her future task as mother and teacher should figure in all school curricula. . . ."

African women know from experience that "a solid religious education is indispensable in order to give girls the basis of natural and Christian law so essential for their lives," and so they "request that all young girls should receive thorough religious instruction in school, after school, outside school, and that, in order to stress the importance of the subject, religious knowledge examinations should be held at least at the end of the girls' school career."

Finally, "considering that the needs of society today call for many and different types of social organizations . . . considering the necessity for woman's active presence on both the social and political levels" in today's Africa, the "seminar participants ask that a knowledge of these problems be given to girls both in school and later on, and to women through adult education." At Nkongsamba, the Camerounian women also stressed education programs for adult women, who "must be encouraged and helped to educate themselves."

These various congresses and seminars underline the fact that African women are becoming even more concerned with their responsibilities and are prepared to discuss their problems before the highest international assemblies.

In December, 1961, the United Nations sponsored a seminar in Addis Ababa on the participation of women in public life. The seminar, organized by the UN secretariat, in cooperation with the government of Ethiopia, was the third of its kind in the regular UN program of advisory services in human rights, the two preceding seminars having been held in Asia and Latin America.

The UN General Assembly had adopted in 1954 a number of recommendations addressed to member states for improving the legal status of African women, and the then colonial administrations charged with implementing them had adopted various measures in that regard. Many of them were never applied, however, either because of the apathy of the local courts or the restraint exercised by public opinion in one or another region firmly opposed to any modification of customary law or tradition. The recommendations and legal measures were, nevertheless, creating a ferment of new thought, which was rapidly gaining ground.

In areas where women were already engaged in social and political activity it was easy to find delegates highly qualified to participate in the Addis-Ababa seminar, which I was privileged to attend as an observer for the World Union of Catholic Women's Organizations and which I found to be particularly interesting and fruitful. There were many truly remarkable personalities among the participants, who for two weeks, under the capable guidance of Mme. Grinberg-Vinaver, chief of the UN Status of Women Section, devoted their serious and concentrated attention to the role of women in public life, the obstacles they encounter in fulfilling that role, and the measures to be taken to overcome the obstacles.

Problems of education received full treatment. Not only the needs of school age children were discussed, but also of those unable to attend school and for whom some form of extra-school or vocational training is urgent. Mass education and community development programs were emphasized, and great attention was given to the need for literacy courses for adult women, so that they no longer need feel inferior either to their husbands who have received some education or to their children currently attending school. But African women are keenly aware that the education of a child begins with his birth, and so they rightly insisted on the education of girls, who are to be the mothers of the future.

Family problems arising from ancient tradition and customary law received special attention. The participants brought experience and practical good sense to a tactful but clear and candid discussion of the painful consequences of some of these customs, such as those involving female circumcision or those which ignore the girl's wishes with respect to her own marriage. They, too, recommend the abolition of female circumcision, child betrothal, child marriages, marriage by exchange and forced marriages. They requested for all women the right to choose a spouse, and the legal recognition of the rights of widows. They also recommended that the bride price have only a symbolic value for if it is too high it is an obstacle to marriage between two people who love each other. Finally, several delegates spoke against polygamy, which almost all of them considered "undesirable and outmoded." Several pointed out that polygamy creates "an environment where rivalry, deceit, and distrust flourish" and that this is a harmful atmosphere for the children. They emphasized the urgent need for legislation which would fix the minimum age for marriage, require the free consent of both spouses, and make the registration of marriages obligatory.

Conscious of the privileges they enjoyed because of their education and social position, the participants stressed as well their responsibilities as educated women toward their less privileged sisters. While keeping all that is good and positive in African tradition, they recognized the necessity

234

of combating poverty and of helping less fortunate women to improve their lot with respect both to home living conditions and to community and national life.

African women are aware that voluntary agencies, the more developed countries, the international organizations, can help them more quickly and effectively to the solution of problems that are enormous of their very nature. With respect to legislative reforms, they place great hope in the influence of the UN Commission on the Status of Women, which took careful note of the conclusions of the seminar and which, in 1960, had drafted a convention on the age of marriage and free consent to be proposed to governments.

"Now," some of my African friends observed, "we can go to work in earnest." They know their task is no small one but they are tackling it with courage and a will to succeed.

Slowly, quietly, but surely, these African women are laying the foundations of a new society which will keep the values of the old African civilizations and will absorb whatever is good in the cultures with which they are now coming in contact. This contact should be greatly developed by giving young African women the opportunity to continue their studies abroad until the educational systems of their own country are expanded. This can be done through scholarship and fellowship programs, by leadership exchange grants, by the friendly welcome accorded African students and visitors so that they may become better acquainted with our world and the way we live, by helping them find solutions to the problems they will meet when they return home.

Not only does Africa need more schools. She needs doctors, hospitals, clinics. Forty per cent of her children die before the age of fifteen, most of them because there is no medical care available in their region.

Intensified exchange and scholarship programs would create a current of sympathy and understanding and would help open up for many African children fuller opportunities for their own future and the future of the countries of which they are citizens.

For true progress, a country needs an educated citizenry that is zealous for that progress. I dream of seeing in every African village a teacher, a social worker, a nurse, who through her dynamic leadership will inspire true community development and in doing so will promote the general well-being of her country.

Conclusion

Often in the intimacy of a heart-to-heart talk about their hopes and problems, I had occasion to ask my African friends the significance of the particular custom that was burdening them.

"That's the way it was when I was born," they would answer simply.

But frequently one would add, "When I am the head of the family I shall not require my people to observe that custom. They will be free to do so or not as they choose."

"Cannot you yourself disregard it now?" I would ask.

"Not yet," was the invariable answer. "It means too much to our mothers, and especially our grandmothers."

This is not peculiarly African. We ourselves are faithful to many customs in Western society whose origin or meaning we would find it hard to explain, and we often observe certain family traditions or practices to please elderly parents or grandparents.

In Africa, where the rhythm of change is accelerating rapidly, the new generations aspire with justification to greater personal freedom, well-being, and happiness for themselves and their children.

They have been born among customs and facilities unfamiliar to "the way it was" when their parents came into the world. They have grown up at a somewhat higher standard of living and amid a degree of material, intellectual, and social progress which until now seemed normal and acceptable but which is no longer sufficient. They desire, with some justice, to attain the same level as the more favored nations, while at the same time they are poring eagerly over their own cultural heritage to take stock of its content.

Contact with other societies that have become too individualistic, that have lost the Christian awareness of their ethic, or are subordinating man to the machine has deepened the Africans' appreciation of the pristine values of their own culture: the fundamentally religious mentality characteristic of them; a sense of awe for what is sacred; respect for God and the Elders; obedience to legitimate authority; cohesive family solidarity; a spirit of mutual help, hospitality, and amiability; a refinement of courtesy in social relationships; a joy of living — that radiates throughout their song and dance.

All these human values can and ought to enrich the cultural patrimony of all mankind and contribute to the rest of the world that basic optimism and joy of living which Africa has managed to preserve throughout her severest trials.

A new African civilization, thrusting its roots deep among the old ancestral values, is taking shape before our eyes. It will probably be less logical, less technical than Western culture, but it will be more intuitive and allow more room for the affective values. It will have "its reasons which reason does not know," for as President Leopold Senghor of Senegal has written: "The African is the child of feeling."

238

CONCLUSION

But at the same time the new African civilization is assimilating the true values of other cultures, and Christian values in particular. This symbiosis, rich in millenary wisdom, sense of community, and enthusiastic youthfulness will add a new star to the various civilizations of the world.